Social Security Disability Guide for Beginners

A Fun and Informative Guide for the Rest of Us

The Foster Law Firm
2345 S Alma School Road
Suite 210
Mesa, AZ 85210
www.fosterlawaz.com

DISCLAIMER

This book is to be used for informational purposes only. It is not to be construed as legal advice. No attorney client relationship has been formed. The legal information in this book is provided "as is" without any representations or warranties, express or implied. Amy Foster makes no representations or warranties in relation to the legal information in this book. Without prejudice to the generality of the foregoing paragraph, Amy Foster does not warrant that the legal information in this book is complete, true, accurate, up-to-date, or non-misleading.

TABLE OF CONTENTS

INTRODUCTION

Welcome to the world of Social Security! I'm here to help people who need benefits but have no clue where to start. Perhaps you're helping a family member or friend who just discovered he or she can't work anymore and is faced with a whole new scary world. Perhaps you just realized you're not going to be able to work again for a long time – perhaps ever. No one ever plans on facing this unless they were a very depressed child. But as you will see – the wild and confusing world of Social Security can be managed and it's not as scary as it seems.

I will tell you right now this book is *not* meant as a guide to help people cheat the federal government. If you bought this book as a how-to guide to get benefits you don't deserve – please go ahead and return it. I'll tell you right now most of my advice is going to boil down to one simple rule - tell the truth. (Although there is a lot more to it than that so read on if you're not a criminal.) If you *are* a criminal my advice just isn't going to work for you. I only ask that you explain why you are returning the book to the bookseller. People handling returns need entertainment too and I can only imagine "I'm returning this book because the author won't help me cheat the government" will brighten someone's day.

A further bit of advice, Mr. or Ms. Potential Criminal, I suggest you look elsewhere for your Master Plan of how to cheat the government. In my years as a Social Security attorney, I have to tell you the reputation of Social Security as a haven for people who are cheating the system is just plain wrong. Social Security knows it has this reputation and if there is even a hint of fraud in your case you will not be winning your case. Sure, the occasional person gets through but it is really rare. Your medical records would need to be spotless and show you had truly severe conditions that severely limit you from work. And quite frankly, if you can fake that why are you bothering with Social Security? I'm sure there are much more profitable cons you could run.

So yes, Social Security's reputation as a hotbed of fraudsters and drug addicts is unwarranted. How do I know this? In 2013, 72,000 cases were reported as disability fraud. Do you know how many got investigated by the Office of the Inspector General after a screening by Social Security? 7,000. That's right. One in ten. And how many actually resulted in charges being pressed? 1,300. Only 1.8% of the cases where people were so sure their neighbor wasn't actually disabled that they reported it to the government were actually found fraudulent[1]. And yet people are so sure that everyone on Social Security doesn't deserve to be there.

---

[1] Source – SSA Inspector General Responds to NOSSCR Conference Questions, NOSSCR Social Security Forum, Volume 36, No. 9, October 2014

This also leads to a great deal of frustration as cases drag on, often for two years or more while people complain to me how "Everyone who's on Social Security doesn't deserve it and here I am in terrible pain and no one believes me!"

So what's going on here? A couple of things. First, the rules change when you turn fifty. If a person has done heavy labor like construction, warehouse work, farming, or anything where a person is lifting a lot of weight regularly - that person is treated differently than the person with a desk job. If the heavy lifter can't do his old job, but can do a job sitting down all day, after turning fifty - he or she wins. After fifty-five, I just have to prove that person can't lift over twenty pounds regularly. This means you might see Joe around the block and he hurt his back and can't do his maintenance job anymore so he's drawing disability. But he's not that bad off physically. He doesn't have to be. Meanwhile, you're waiting for your disability benefits to come through for two years and you can't get out of bed. The standards are different.

Second, different conditions are sometimes treated differently. Conditions that are easy to diagnose, can easily be seen in test results, or can be seen with our own two eyes (i.e., an amputation) can win faster than ones we can't see. Migraines, fibromyalgia, multiple sclerosis, strokes and mental disorders can take longer to win because they rely on what we tell our doctors versus what our doctors observe. Family members, friends and neighbors may also not see those conditions as severe if they cannot see those conditions as clearly as some other conditions. Which leads me to what I think is the number one issue.

No one really knows your situation but you. Think about the last person you know who you said shouldn't be on disability. (Or who someone else said shouldn't be on disability.) Now, whether or not that's true, have you seen the medical records? Do you spend all day together? Have you seen him on his worst day? Have you gone to doctor's appointments with him and heard what the doctor said? 99% of the time, people are talking about a neighbor or a friend or an acquaintance but not someone they know intimately. It's someone they see at the mailbox or someone they see only when that person is "feeling up to it". This means they see that person on the absolute best day that person is having and the rest of the time they assume that person is feeling the same. It may have taken all the energy that person had that week to talk to you at the mailbox for five minutes. You just don't know.

The news has convinced people that everyone on Social Security Disability benefits is faking or lazy. This means that when people apply they have a huge amount of shame to overcome when in fact they are applying for benefits they have paid for. It's no different than applying for a pension early due to disability. Now it's true that it's more difficult to get because there's not enough money. That's a political issue and not the purpose of this book[2]. Regardless, when you apply for Social Security Disability benefits, you are *not* applying for welfare[3]. It is the same money as when you pay for your retirement taxes. So relax. Come with me to explore the exciting world of Social Security[4]...

---

[2] I promise the web is full of information about Social Security funding. If you really want to go down that rabbit hole, go for it.

[3] There is a need-based disability benefit and we'll discuss that as well.

[4] Or as exciting as I can make it. It's still government benefits.

CHAPTER ONE: "WAIT! WHAT AM I APPLYING FOR AGAIN?" THE DIFFERENT TYPES OF SOCIAL SECURITY BENEFITS

Before you even apply for Social Security, you need to know what you're applying for. Sounds easy, right? Well, kind of. Let's start with the easy parts.

There's no partial disability. That's right. We're talking all or nothing.

It's not disease specific. It's whether you're disabled as a whole. Throw everything in that might affect your ability to work. If you develop new conditions after you apply, toss those on in there too. Back problems, depression, diabetes, and hey, your medication makes you sunburn easily! Tell Social Security all about it. If you don't mention it — it doesn't exist.

You need to have stopped working. It's not quite this simple, and we'll discuss whether you can work part-time in another chapter, but if you're still working full time you are not ready to apply.

They're not going to pay you while you wait for your benefits to come through. No, I don't know what they expect you to do while you wait. People definitely do go into debt, go bankrupt, lose their houses, and even live on the streets while waiting for Social Security. Please try not to let that happen to you. I'll have a chapter about possible resources for you near the end of the book.

There are a bunch of different types of benefits and they will give you a headache thinking about all of them. I know this because they give me a headache and I've been doing this for a very long time. I put the most important first and feel free to skip ahead. Here's a little trick — if you don't know what to apply for, you can always do one of two things.

- Call your nice neighborhood Social Security attorney and tell them your situation. You will be given advice. Free consultations are standard.

- Call your *local*[5] Social Security office and when you apply, they will sign you up for the right type of benefits.

In all seriousness, I do think it's important to understand what you're applying for and why. You don't have to understand every detail, but the process will be far smoother and you're less likely to panic about the process if you understand what you're asking for. Isn't that why you're reading this book?

---

[5] Always call your local office and not the national 1-800 number which is 1-800-722-1213. The local office can give you better information and they pick up the phone faster. I cannot stress this enough.

Retirement

It's not why we're here, but it is by far the most common type of benefit for Social Security. When you work, you pay FICA taxes, which is the Federal Insurance Contributions Act. It's part of your payroll tax and it funds Social Security and Medicare. The more you work, the more you pay into the system. If you don't work, you don't qualify for retirement or Medicare. The more you make, the more you contribute, and the more you get! If you make a lot of money, you pay the maximum amount, and you stop having to pay FICA taxes for the rest year.

And what do they mean by work? It's the government! Of course they have an answer for that. Working a day at McDonald's and quitting is not going to cut it. You need to earn what they call "quarters of coverage". But what it really means is you had to earn $1220 four times in each year[6] (or $4880 a year) to be covered each year. You need to have ten years worth of work to retire.

People can get into trouble here if they didn't pay taxes on their income. This is also known as getting paid "under the table". See, if you don't pay taxes, you don't get the benefit of having paid those taxes. Fair enough?

Depending on the year you were born, you can get early retirement starting at age 62 and full retirement starting at age 67. The amount you get paid for early retirement is reduced. The later you were born, the later the ages for early and late retirement.

This table will tell you when your early and late retirement age is and what reduction there is for deciding to retire early.
http://www.ssa.gov/oact/quickcalc/earlyretire.html.

Truthfully, people generally do not have problems with retirement. No one ever needs my help. It just isn't that hard. You can apply online at

---

[6]As of 2016. It changes every year.

http://www.ssa.gov/planners/about.htm. The only issue I ever see is if someone has had their Social Security number stolen and their earnings record isn't correct. The real trouble comes up next.

DISABILITY BENEFITS

There are two major types of Social Security disability benefits. Social Security Disability benefits (SSDI) and Supplemental Security Insurance benefits (SSI). We'll handle SSDI first. But before you get really confused, let's make this really simple.

If you don't know whether you should apply for SSDI benefits or SSI benefits, just apply for them both! There is absolutely nothing wrong with this. Both applications will proceed together through the Social Security system just fine. Social Security will let you know if you don't qualify for one or the other. As long as you qualify financially for one of them, you're fine.

Social Security Disability Benefits (SSDI)

SSDI benefits are the major form of disability benefit. They are what you pay for out of your FICA taxes and the amount you get is based off of how much you worked. The amount can be as low as $300 or as high as $2,639.[7] But you have to have paid into the system to receive the benefit.

Generally, you have to have worked five out of the past ten years before you became disabled to get SSDI benefits. It's the same idea as having to have worked ten years to get retirement benefits. You need to have earned at least $5040 a year or 40 quarters of coverage. So if I became disabled in 2015, I had to have worked at least from 2006 to 2010 and made the minimum amount of quarters of coverage in each year.

---

[7] http://www.ssa.gov/news/press/factsheets/colafacts2016.pdf

So why do you want this SSDI benefit so much? Two reasons. It can pay a lot more than SSI and you get Medicare! SSI recipients cannot get Medicare benefits. But if you qualify for SSDI benefits, Medicare starts two years and the sixth month after the date they find you disabled. The difference in medical care alone is a reason many people file for disability. Plus money is nice.

How do you know how much you get? Social Security used to send out statements once a year telling you how much you'd get if you retired today and how much you'd get if you became disabled today. Those were accurate. They stopped sending those out a few years ago. You can now get your earnings statement online at http://www.ssa.gov/myaccount/. The benefit calculators are online at http://www.ssa.gov/planners/benefitcalculators.htm#sb=3

Supplemental Security Insurance (SSI)

If SSDI is so great, why does anyone bother with SSI? Well, sometimes people haven't worked enough. Sometimes people haven't worked at all. SSI is closer to what people think of as welfare and is paid out of a completely different fund than SSDI. It is *not* paid for out of FICA taxes.

Before anyone gets on their high horse about people being too lazy to work and starts writing me nasty emails, let's also remember that SSI is also for people who are disabled from birth, who are never able to live on their own and their families don't have enough money to provide for them. Those children would be out on the street without this program.

SSI pays a maximum of $733 for 2016[8]. This is why I said you can and should apply for both SSI and SSDI. If

---

[8] http://www.ssa.gov/oact/cola/SSI.html

SSDI is only paying you $500, you can get SSDI and the wonderful Medicare benefits and have SSI make up the difference in pay.

Both SSDI and SSI have the same disability standards that we will discuss at length in the rest of the book. Your case does not move any faster whether you file for SSDI or SSI. But to get SSI, you also have to be really needy. Practically speaking, 99% of the time, my clients know if they qualify or not. They either say "Oh no, we have money in the bank and my spouse is working." Or they say, "We have nothing! Sign us up!" But just in case you're in the 1%, here's how it works.

Basically, you're allowed $2000 in cash if you're single and $3000 if you're married. They do *not count:*

- the home you live in and the land it is on;

- Household goods and personal effects (e.g., your wedding and engagement rings, furniture, clothes, etc.);

- burial spaces for you or your immediate family;

- burial funds for you and your spouse, each valued at $1,500 or less

- life insurance policies with a combined face value of $1,500 or less;

- one vehicle, regardless of value, if it is used for transportation for you or a member of your household;

- retroactive SSI or Social Security benefits for up to nine months after you receive them (including payments received in installments);

- Grants, scholarships, fellowships, or gifts set aside to pay educational expenses for 9 months after receipt[9].

This also means your spouse can work, but your income and savings need to stay below the SSI amount.

If you have more than one car for your family, you need to sell a car and spend down the amount to get you below the amount needed to qualify for SSI. It does not matter if the car is a clunker and not worth anything! In fact, it

[9] http://www.ssa.gov/ssi/text-resources-ussi.htm

doesn't matter if the car doesn't run! I speak from experience. The car is what messes most people up. Get rid of the car.

It is also a really bad idea to apply for SSI to see if you pass and then figure you'll do some fiddling with your finances later and then try again. I agree that it seems like that should work. But the government does not want to play that game with you. They see that as trying to defraud the government[10]. You'd need to wait two years before you try again and I don't think you want to do that. Try to get your ducks in a row before you apply.

You're also not allowed to give away all of your stuff just to qualify for SSI. If you have two cars and you "give" it to your friend so the title is in your friend's name but you're still driving that car, they consider that fraud. They check for recent sales and transfers of title if they

---

[10] Please don't try to defraud the government. It's never a good use of your time.

think something's fishy. If you think you're on the borderline for assets, just talk to an attorney. Again, free consultations are standard.

This should go without saying but do *not* get divorced to qualify for SSI! This also comes up surprisingly often. One half of the couple is working and making too much money, so they figure they'll get divorced so the other half can get SSI. All I can tell you is that SSA is well aware that this happens and they check to see if the couple is still living at the same address. They may send someone out to see who's living at that house. I had one case where the couple actually did get divorced but the husband was just lazy and didn't change his address. His wife had a terrible time proving she wasn't trying to fool anyone and actually was divorced. If you get divorced so one half of the couple can get SSI, be prepared to live apart and actually be divorced.

The other reason why SSDI is more desirable than SSI is because if you receive SSI, you have to do some accounting. SSI is only supposed to be used for food and shelter. No, I don't know what they expect you to do for clothes and toothpaste. That's why it's called *Supplemental* Security Income. You have to show that it's only being used for food and shelter. We'll go over it more in the chapter on what to do if you get awarded. Just keep it in mind.

Now, it's around this time, that I have a lot of family members say, "Amy, I can't afford to support my kid forever, but I want to leave them *something*. SSI pays nothing! What if my little guy has an emergency?" Good news! We plan for that! SSI really doesn't pay a lot. It's really fantastic when you have nothing. $733 is a fortune when you're living on the street or close to it. It can get you a place to live and food to eat. But if you're looking at a lifetime of $733 a month, Great Aunt

Harriett may want to leave you something in her will or family members may want to help out. If you're receiving SSDI, it doesn't matter. You can have millions in the bank because there's no income requirement. But with SSI, since it's need-based, you need to be...needy.

So Social Security devised the special needs trust. A trust is basically just a system where money is legally held by someone else for a period of time. In this case, the disabled person cannot hold money in his own name. In this case, another person is the trustee and can distribute money for special things – televisions, medical needs, dentist visits, special treats, etc. They have to be set up very specifically so the disabled person can still qualify for SSI. These are great solutions for kids who are disabled from birth whose parents want them taken care of.

There's one thing I want you to do for me if you decide to use one of these. Please use someone who specializes in doing special needs trusts! Don't just use your regular attorney who does wills. These are complicated and you really need someone who knows exactly how to do these. It is so much cheaper than trying to fix the trust later. I speak from experience. Just do it right the first time.

If SSDI gets Medicare, what does SSI get? You get your state's version of Medicare, which is generally referred to as Medicaid. Nice and confusing terms. In California it's MediCAL, in Arizona it's AHCCCCS. Every state has their own name for it. A bunch of states are now lumped in under Obamacare. It's never going to be as good as Medicare, but it's insurance. If you have your own insurance through the healthcare marketplace, you can opt out. I'm a big fan of having more options in insurance than not enough so just know that you have other options for insurance[11].

OTHER BENEFITS

And now we enter the poorly understood realm of the "other benefits". All are good to know about. Most will not apply to you. Feel free to skim at your leisure because you may find out that you or someone you know may be missing out on some money.

CHILDREN'S BENEFITS

There are a few types so childrens' benefits get far more confusing than they should be. When talking to your attorney or Social Security office, you need to really clear why your child may be getting benefits. Is it because *you* are disabled or because *your child* is disabled?

If you qualify for SSDI and you have children, you can receive some extra money up to your family maximum. What is your family maximum? Remember when I

---

[11] See Chapter Thirteen on resources for disabled people.

showed you the Social Security calculator and how to get your benefit statement a couple pages back? It's on there. If you're getting SSI, you're out of luck. This applies to SSDI only. Your children need to be:

- under age 18; **or**
- 18-19 years old and a full-time student (no higher than grade 12); **or**
- 18 or older **and** have a disability that started before age 22[12].

Grandchildren can count too, if you are providing the sole support for them. Adopted kids are covered, of course.

Where it gets tricky, is if the parents are divorced. If you're not supporting your kids, you do not get money for them. Which is fair. But what if you're not supporting your kids because you had no money? And you owe back child support? (Fun fact - they will withhold your SSDI back pay for child support if you have a judgment against you!) What if your kids are not

[12] http://www.ssa.gov/dibplan/dfamily4.htm

with you because they're being held by Child Protective Services? If your child is being held by the state or in foster care, you're not supporting them so you do not get child's benefits. If your child is with the other parent and you owe child support, you'll get child's benefits, but the check will go to the other parent.

Stepchildren are also usually included in the benefits as well as long as you are supporting them. The easiest way to think about all of this is if you are supporting the child, you can claim the child.

It all gets really complicated. You might want to talk to your family law attorney for this one. Definitely bring a copy of your divorce decree when you fill out your child benefits form. You have to go in to the Social Security office anyway to file for childrens' benefits. This is not something you can do online. You will need a certified copy of the child's birth certificate. Tell the Social

Security worker what your situation is and they will know what to do.

DISABLED CHILD'S BENEFITS

Children can get benefits if they are disabled and under the age 18. The child can either get SSI or SSDI. Right now you're thinking, "Of course the child can get SSI, what child has money?" But it's the *parents* that need to meet the financial requirements. Hence, it's a bit trickier.

To get SSDI benefits, the child must have a parent who is disabled, retired or dead. The child is then entitled to half of the amount the parent would receive at full retirement age once he meets the disability requirements[13]. If you qualify for SSDI, and your child is disabled, start that paperwork right away for your child.

SSI benefits are a little more difficult because the parents need to meet the SSI requirements. The parents are

[13] http://www.ssa.gov/pubs/EN-05-10085.pdf

allowed to have a bit more money. The limit is $3424 for one parent in the household and $4158 for a two parent household in 2016[14]. All other SSI requirements apply.

Once the child reaches 18, the benefits are cut off and the child then needs to apply for adult disability benefits. The disability standards for children are different as well because the adult standards are all about whether the person can work. We really aren't concerned about whether a toddler can work.

ADULT DISABLED CHILD BENEFITS

If you have a child who becomes disabled before he turns 22, this is the category you really want to pay attention to. If a parent dies or starts receiving retirement, the disabled child can receive benefits on his parent's earnings if you prove he is disabled before he turned 22.

---

[14] http://www.socialsecurity.gov/ssi/text-child-ussi.htm

You don't have to prove it before he actually turns 22. You can prove it later on. Just make sure you can prove it happened before he turned 22. Then he can get up to 50% of his parent's retirement benefit. This can be more than the SSI amount and you don't have to deal with any accounting or special needs trusts. If the child is already receiving SSI from when he was 22 this can be very easy. Otherwise you need a really good medical record. If you think this is going to be an issue for your child, just get a copy of the medical records when your child is in his early twenties and hang on to them.

WIDOW'S BENEFITS

If you have a deceased spouse, pay attention! You can catch a break! And it's about time since it sounds like you need one. Once you turn 50, you can file for disability under your deceased spouse's Social Security number and get half his benefit. Even better, once you turn 60, you can just go ahead and file for retirement and get the same deal.

If you were divorced at the time of death, you can still get the benefit if you were married more than ten years. It's called widow's benefits but this works for men, too. This was designed for women who stayed home with the children while their husbands worked. Then the men dropped dead and the women were left with nothing and no earnings and had no retirement built up. But it's 2016 and if you can make more money under this rule - go for it! Besides, your spouse paid into the system for this benefit and someone should be using it.

Children of the deceased who are under 18 are also eligible to receive benefits. The total amount a family can receive is 150% of the benefit the deceased was eligible to get. It really is easiest just to go to your local office and file for this benefit.

If a person dies and has children under 18, they can get some help from Social Security. If the surviving spouse is taking care of children under 16, she can get money as well[15]. The total amount a family can receive is 150% of the benefit the deceased was eligible to get at full retirement. I know this gets confusing. It really is easiest just to go to your local office, give them your information and see what you can get.

There is also a one-time death payment of $255 as long as the person has worked long enough. Just go down to the local office with the death certificate. No one seems to know about this benefit so tell people about it! I think it exists so Social Security gets notified when people die and there's less fraud with Social Security payments. Nevertheless, money is money so pass it on!

---

[15] http://www.ssa.gov/pubs/EN-05-10084.pdf

Now that I've given you all headaches from the different types of benefits and how they all work together, you really just need to remember two things:

- You can apply for more than one type of benefit at a time, and

- Your attorney and Social Security can guide you to what you should be applying for.

Now, on to how all of this actually works!

Chapter Two: "How do I get them to believe me?" Standards of Disability

You know you're disabled and can't work. You're in constant pain. You sleep all the time or not at all. Every day is a constant struggle. But how do you convince Social Security of that? Unfortunately, they are not going to believe you just because you're charming and a nice person. You're going to have to prove it.

What does disability even mean, anyway?

In short, it means you can't work. To be a bit more detailed, it means you can't earn more than $1130 a month[16] which Social Security calls Substantial Gainful

---

[16] This number is as of 2016. The number changes every year due to cost of living. For the current year's amount see http://www.socialsecurity.gov/oact/cola/sga.html.

Activity. Practically speaking if you're working and earning right below the allowed amount, Social Security will likely wonder why you couldn't work an extra hour or two and be over the amount. People do need money and to support their families so you need to do what you have to do. Just be aware that the more money you earn, the harder it will be to prove that you're disabled. You do not need to worry about pensions, stock dividends, long or short term disability, state disability benefits or any other money coming in that does not actually come from you working for this part of the analysis.

You also need to prove that you are not able to work due to a *medical* condition. Simply not working is not enough. Your medical condition needs to be severe enough that it will keep you out of work for at least twelve months or result in your death[17]. This doesn't mean that you're limited to just one medical condition. It

[17] http://www.ssa.gov/dibplan/dqualify4.htm.

can be a combination of medical conditions. Say your neck injury isn't quite enough to keep you off work for a year, but you also had a knee replacement surgery that went poorly and the combination will keep you out of work for a year. That will be enough.

You also do not need to be off work for a year before you apply. If your doctor thinks you will be off for at least year, you should go ahead and apply for benefits now. Disability benefits can take a long time to process and there's no point sitting around waiting for the year to pass. If Social Security thinks you may not meet the year requirement, they will cheerfully deny you and wait to see if you improve. At least your case will be moving through the system in the meantime. You may get lucky and get approved the first time.

If you think you'll only be off a couple of months, definitely wait to apply. The system is crowded and

Social Security will not pay a claimant whose medical condition is only supposed to last less than a year. That knee surgery that will keep you down for a few weeks is not a great reason to file for benefits. You will hear this again and again from me, but talk to your doctor if you are unsure.

PROVING THE DISABILITY

Each condition is different, but you're going to need your doctor's support no matter what. This means you're going to need to go to the doctor regularly. For some reason I have lots of people come and talk to me who tell me how sick they are but haven't been to a doctor for years. If you want disability, you need to get medical treatment. Fortunately, because of Obamacare, insurance is no longer the issue it used to be. You need to go to the doctor and you need to follow all recommendations.

Social Security needs to know how you are doing and if you are doing everything you can to improve your health.

This does not mean that you have to have back surgery if you don't want to have back surgery. You have a right to direct your own medical treatment. It does mean that you need to check your blood sugars and take your insulin if you're diabetic and stay on your psychiatric medications if you have mental health issues[18].

You also need to keep seeing a doctor. I understand that a condition can be stable and there's not much a doctor can do. But if a condition is not in the medical records for treatment, I can't use it in court as a reason that you can't work. So go to the doctor. Social Security will hold it against you if you go several months without treatment[19].

---

[18] If you do not want to do a medical treatment for religious reasons or you have valid personal reasons that's fine. You just shouldn't refuse to take medicine in the hopes that you will deteriorate and then can get on disability.

It is very important to have a good relationship with your doctor so keep the lines of communication open. Even if your doctor does not want to complete forms, you do *not* want your doctor fighting your disability. You will lose and there won't be much your attorney can do about it.

I cannot count the number of times I go to the doctor and tell them what I do and the doctor instantly launches into a story about the patients who aren't disabled and want disability paperwork filled out. All doctors are on the lookout for people who are faking disability. I know *you* are not faking disability and *you're* reading this book so you can have the best chance of getting disability, so relax. Just know that your doctor is probably very defensive about any patient asking about going on disability. Try to respect that and your doctor will be much more receptive.

---

[19] There may be valid reasons for this like lack of insurance or financial reasons. We understand. Go as often as you can.

If you can, try to stay with the same doctor as long as possible. A long treating history goes a long way with Social Security. I know that's not always possible with insurance changes and it's not the end of the world if you have to change doctors. If you can, try to cultivate a good relationship with your doctor. You don't need to suck up or bring the doctor presents, just remember that the doctor's opinion matters. If you can, before you stop working, discuss it with your doctor. You don't need to demand, "I'm going on disability, will you screw that up?" But instead, maybe say, "Doctor, I'm having a really hard time at work. Do you think I should be working? Should I take some time off?"

It is very important to know whether your doctor is going to support your disability. I'm not saying it happens often, but there have been incidents where a patient's doctor has written directly to Social Security or an Administrative Law Judge telling them that the patient is not disabled and is faking a condition. Just imagine the effect that has on a case. Your life is much easier if you discuss going on disability with your doctor before you stop working and before you file. The doctor will feel like his opinion is worth something and you'll know if your doctor will support you. Your doctor will also realize how sick you're feeling and may look for medical options he wasn't willing to try before.

You should also ask if there are limitations you should be following. We love to have doctors fill out forms for what the claimant can and can't do physically. Doctors hate filling them out. It's okay to say, "Hey doctor, how much should I be lifting? How long should I be on my feet?" Then ask the doctor to write that down in the medical record. Also, just ask if your doctor will fill out forms for you. Make sure you ask the doctor, not his staff. It will be harder for the doctor to say no to your face.

If at all possible, try to see a doctor, not a Nurse

Practitioner or a Physician's Assistant. Social Security

does not give them the same weight as a medical doctor.

I think that rule is unfair and I have the highest respect

for Nurse Practitioners and Physician's Assistants

because I know some absolutely fantastic ones. But if all

you can see is a Nurse Practitioner or Physician's

Assistant, then by all means do so. Do not avoid medical

care because you cannot see a doctor. You will still

receive excellent care. If you're given limitations by the

Nurse Practitioner or Physician's Assistant, or they fill

out forms, have the doctor just sign off on it and you will

be fine.

I know that a lot of my recommendations require

participation from your doctor and the opportunity to

actually go see a doctor regularly which may not be

possible. This is the best case scenario. Do what you

can. What I am saying is that if you have the opportunity

to go to the doctor, please go. Please don't stop going to the doctor for a year and a half then complain how you were denied because you are so sick. You need evidence and that evidence comes from going to the doctor. Even if your condition is stable you should schedule check-ups.

WHAT SORT OF CONDITIONS ARE WE LOOKING FOR?

In short, we want anything that limits your ability to work. I see people get hung up on diagnoses all the time. I get calls all the time where someone says, "I got diagnosed with diabetes, am I disabled?" How should I know? What are your symptoms? You could have a small brain tumor and be just fine. You could also have dry skin and be completely disabled because the skin cracks and bleeds constantly causing massive pain and sanitary problems in the workplace. The diagnosis is important, but we really care how it affects you.

I've had a number of cases where we didn't even have a good diagnosis. Multiple sclerosis and lupus are horrible to diagnose and a person can be terribly incapacitated for a long time before the diagnosis is confirmed. Some conditions are rare and we don't have a diagnosis before we get the claimant disability. We have to go off of the symptoms. Those cases aren't necessarily easy to win, but if the symptoms are bad enough, we certainly can win.

Most cases we see are back injuries because it is very difficult to sit, stand or walk with a back problem. You can't work if you can't sit, stand or walk a total of eight hours a day. We also see a number of mental health cases, diabetes, heart issues, and lung problems. Almost no one has just one condition they're claiming disability for. Nor should they. You should mention anything that would limit your ability to work. You have allergies? Throw it in. Medications make you sensitive to sunlight?

Throw it in. Poor eyesight? Throw it in. Carpal Tunnel? Throw it in. Anything that would eliminate a job should be included. Cases are won all the time on how much a person can use his hands or how much he can lift. It does no good to mention to your attorney after the hearing that you can't do that cleaner job because you can't be around dust and fumes if you never mentioned it before. Bring up everything.

Medication side effects are also important. If you have to be on a medication to keep you alive but it makes you sleep half the day and lose your memory, you really need to mention that. If you're losing weight because you're throwing up constantly from your medication, bring it up to Social Security. You can't work if you're throwing up constantly or sleeping half the day. Your doctor should probably be aware of the side effects so mention it to him as well. The side effects should be well documented in the record.

SOCIAL SECURITY LISTINGS

Social Security has what are called listings and they are basically what they sound like. They're a list of conditions and if you have them to a specific severity, you get disability. For example, if you have epilepsy and you have grand mal seizures more than once a month and you can't control it with medication, then you get disability[20]. Listings exist for most conditions in one form or another. You have to be really sick to meet a listing.

The listings are really technical and filled with medical jargon. They're fairly miserable for anyone who doesn't speak medical. But if you meet one, it should mean that you automatically qualify for disability. In practice, we spend a lot of time arguing that someone meets a listing and we need doctors' opinions that a listing is met. You

[20]http://www.ssa.gov/disability/professionals/bluebook/11.00-Neurological-Adult.htm#11_02

can find the listings at

http://www.ssa.gov/disability/professionals/bluebook/AdultListings.htm. It might be easiest to bring a copy of your listing to your doctor and ask if you meet it. For example, if you had back problems, you'd bring the listings for 1.00 which is the Musculoskeletal system.

You need to know the listings exist, because they may come up in your hearing and it's nice to know if you meet one. However, you probably can't determine if you meet a listing on your own. You can request Social Security look at a specific listing, but a doctor must find you meet one.

What you can do is print out the listing for your condition and bring it to your doctor and ask if you meet it. If your doctor thinks you do, have him write a letter to Social Security.

This is all fine, but what happens when you have a really serious illness and you don't have two years to wait for Social Security to make a decision? What about the people with terminal cancer? Surely there are some people who are so obviously disabled that they don't need to jump through all these hoops, right?

Yes, there is a way around some of this. If you are terminally ill, Social Security has an expedited track to get your disability approved. Those cases are called "TERI cases" for "terminal illness". Your case can be designated as a TERI case if your condition is "a medical condition that is untreatable and expected to result in death[21]". If this is you, you can ask that your case be designated a TERI case or Social Security can do it on

---

[21] https://secure.ssa.gov/poms.nsf/lnx/0423020045

their own. Your case is then supposed to be resolved within 60 days.

If you're not sure whether or not your case should be designated a TERI case, go ahead and ask. The worst that happens is that your case gets reviewed and then gets put back with the other cases.

If you find out midway through your case that you've been diagnosed with a terminal illness, you can ask that your case be designated a TERI case at any time.

There are other conditions that meet what we call a "compassionate allowance". It's a list of conditions that are so severe that the diagnosis alone obviously meets the definition of disability. One condition is ALS or Lou Gehrig's disease where the condition is so severe and degenerative that once you have the diagnosis, you're clearly disabled. The list of compassionate allowance conditions can be found here:

http://www.ssa.gov/compassionateallowances/conditions.

htm. You just need proof that you have the disease in order to get disability. Be sure that you can show however the disease is diagnosed to Social Security. A letter from your doctor is likely not enough.

OTHER WAYS OF PROVING DISABILITY

If you don't meet a listing, you then have to prove that you can't do any job. People often think that if they can't do their old job, then they're disabled. That's not true. I regularly have to tell people how just because they can no longer be a doctor or a construction worker they still need to see if there's something else they can do. Just because you may not be able to concentrate or do heavy work like you used to, we still need to see if there are other jobs available.

Now to be fair, its jobs that you can do *right now*. This means we're looking at a lot of unskilled jobs. Social Security isn't interested in jobs you could do with training. They're also jobs that need to exist in large numbers in your area. That one job that exists a thousand miles away that only two people in the world do but you might be able to do? We're not looking at that. What if you live in the middle of nowhere where there are no jobs? Bad news. Social Security has a very big idea of what your area is. You're not going to win your case by moving. Their idea of "area" is generally state-wide[22].

We're also not looking at friendly employers who let you get away with everything. Let's say at your last job your boss let you lie down in his office with the lights off every time you had a migraine. You really can't count on every boss letting you do that. Social Security plans on bosses being strict with no extra breaks, no extra time off, and they expect you to keep up with the other employees. If your disability is going to make you slow down, spend

---

[22] Unless you live in a tiny state, then they'll expand to several states. Sorry, Rhode Island.

all your time in the bathroom, or miss several days a month, you're in luck! You have a pretty good case.

When you're talking to your lawyer or Social Security, it's really important to mention any medical condition that's going to affect these things. I know it's not fun to talk about your bathroom habits, but I win a lot of cases because people have to spend a lot of time in the bathroom. Also mention *anything* that would limit jobs where you have to be around fumes, smoke, dust, or even be outside. Social Security loves to tell you that you can do jobs like laundry sorter, small parts assembler and parking garage ticket taker. All these jobs involve factories or being around fumes and dust. Something you may not think is a big deal may end up being making all the difference in your case. Speak up. If I have to prove you can't do any job, I need all the ammunition I can get. I really don't mind winning on something minor and neither should you.

PHYSICAL LIMITATIONS

Physical limitations are our bread and butter. It all comes down to some very simple factors: How long can you sit, stand and walk and how much can you lift?

Because most of our cases are back cases, Social Security rules are built around sitting, standing and walking. It's very difficult to find a job if you can't sit, stand or walk some combination of eight hours a day. No jobs (at least according to Social Security) are going to let you lay down on the job. You, or your doctor, are going to need to think about how much you can sit, stand and walk. Both at one time and in an eight hour day.

Here's where it gets hard because I'm aware that you're sitting there thinking "It depends on the day! I have good days and bad days!" Social Security's forms don't account for the days you can't get out of bed or have to lie down more. I know it changes every day and it's going to change on your activity.

It also needs to be what you can do *comfortably*. And I don't mean with no pain because that's probably never going to be the case. I mean with no additional pain and where you won't be in any extra pain later. We really want to know what you could do day in and day out because that's what you would have to do at a job.

Estimate how long you can sit, stand and walk at one time on a normal day. Not on your best day, but also not on your worst day. Then estimate about how much you can do in an eight hour day. Make very, very clear what happens on a bad day. Do you need to elevate your legs? How high? Do you nap? Are you laying down? For how long? If you're walking, how long do you need to stop and rest for?

We also need to be very careful about what we consider sitting. I am not talking about sitting in your comfy recliner with lots of padding and pillows. Social Security wants to know how long you can sit at a job. We are talking about an office chair (at best) with your feet on the floor. Your arms may or may not have an arm rest. Changes things, doesn't it?

You also need to have a decent idea of how much you can lift. Social Security tends to think of lifting in ten pound increments. Unless you are a bowler or a weight lifter, most of us don't have any idea of how much things weigh. In hearings, I almost always use a gallon of milk as a reference. A gallon of milk is eight pounds. We also talk about bags of groceries, a case of soda (a 24 pack of soda is about 20 pounds), bags of dog food, etc. Often people know how much children, grandchildren or pets weigh and use that as a reference.

Do NOT hurt yourself trying to see how much you can lift! Your doctor may or may not have told you how much you should be lifting. If you've been off work long enough to be applying for disability, you should have a good idea of your limitations. You know if you can easily lift a gallon of milk, if it takes two hands, and if you can carry it across the kitchen.

Social Security also limits lifting to whether you can lift a weight occasionally or frequently. Occasionally is defined as a third of the day and frequently is defined as two-thirds of the day. When you say you can lift something, you need to be clear about how easy it is to lift it. If you say it's "no problem" to lift a case of soda, be aware that Social Security might take that to mean that you could carry it around all day. Be specific. Can you lift it just once? Or can you do it multiple times?

There are other factors Social Security pays attention to. We look at climbing stairs, ramps, and ladders. Whether you can crouch, stoop, bend, reach overhead, handle and finger with your hands, see, hear, be exposed to fumes and dust, and be around temperature extremes to name just a few. I cannot stress this enough – please list any impairment you have that would keep you from performing a job – any job.

Of course there are a number of medical conditions that just aren't going to fit into the sit/stand/walk framework. It's fine. We win those cases constantly. It just means that we need to handle those a little differently. Heart conditions, liver problems, lung problems and fibromyalgia are all cases that I have come across my desk constantly that can't be boiled down to a simple sit/stand/walk formula. With these cases I really want to know about fatigue. How long can you do anything before you get tired? If you're having pain, where are

you having pain? How often do you need to rest? Are
you having swelling anywhere? For heart conditions are
you feeling your heart beat irregularly? Are you getting
chest pain? What brings it on? If you have lung issues,
are you using a breathing machine or inhaler and if so,
how often? What makes you short of breath? We spend
a lot of time looking at lab results for these cases.
Particularly in heart, lung and liver cases, these might be
the situations when you bring the listings to your doctor
and ask if you meet any of them. For fibromyalgia, we
want to know about trigger points, gastric issues, and
fatigue. For all of these cases, it's a good idea to keep a
diary of your fatigue and your activity level. We want to
know how long it takes to recover after activities.

If you have migraines or seizures, the sit/stand/walk
formula really doesn't apply to you and the fatigue issue
may not either. Except when you have the migraines or
seizures, you may feel just fine. But if you have the

migraines or seizures often enough, work may be out of the question for you. Look again at the listings for seizures to see if you qualify. Social Security tends to agree that if you miss more than two days a month unexpectedly for your illness, you're going to be unemployable. Therefore, you want to keep a good record of your seizures and migraines and how long they last. I also want to know how long it took to recover afterwards. Keep track of the medicines you've tried. If you've gone to the emergency room for seizures or migraines, please tell your attorney and/or Social Security! Even if treatment isn't helping, please keep going to the doctor, at least while your case is active. It's really hard to win your case with no new medical records. Besides, there are new treatments available all the time, so you never know when one might work for you.

MENTAL LIMITATIONS

You should also include any mental limitations you may have such as problems with concentration, memory loss, mood swings or problems with crowds. This is nothing to be ashamed of. I cannot stress this enough. If you're applying for Social Security disability, then you've probably had a pretty rough time of it lately. Most of my clients are on some sort of anti-depressant and I'm happy they are. There's nothing wrong with saying to your doctor, "Hey, my life has changed drastically and I'm having a hard time dealing with it. Can I please have some help here?"

There's even a specific diagnosis for exactly this situation. It's called Adjustment Disorder and basically it's when you've had a major life event and you're having trouble adjusting to it. Sometimes it turns into depression, and sometimes it doesn't. Depression is real and it's not something you can just snap out of. If it were, antidepressants wouldn't work. Don't be afraid to talk to your doctor. Your family and friends (and friendly Social Security attorney) will thank you for it.

What we really care about for disability purposes is attention and concentration. Depression and anxiety are going to cause a decrease in attention and concentration but pain and pain medicine are going to do this as well. Again, it all comes back to symptoms. You might be hallucinating all day long but if you can ignore it and do your work then you're not disabled.

You also need to be able to finish the job at hand. If you find yourself starting chores or projects but never finishing them, or finishing them days later, then you need to tell your doctor. It does not do an employer any good to have an employee who can't finish the work.

Really pay attention (if you can) to how long you can do something. Ask a friend or family member what they notice. Can you watch a television program all the way through? Is it a half an hour or hour long program? What about a movie? Do you remember what happened? Can you follow the plot? What about television plots from week to week? Do you read books? Do you have to reread what you read before? Can you remember to take your medication? Do you need to set alarms? Do you remember appointments?

Social Security also cares about how well you get along with others. There are some positions like night janitors where you really don't have to deal with other people. But to even get those jobs you have supervisors and you're going to need to interview. Every job has some degree of interpersonal contact and if a mental illness is so severe that you cannot get along with anyone to get hired, you can't work. You need to get along well enough with your supervisors and co-workers to do your job. Even if it's just on a superficial level you have to have interpersonal contact.

You really need to spend some time thinking about how much time you spend with others and what you're doing. Do you see friends? How do you see them? Are you talking on the phone? Going to lunch? Do you go to movies? Do crowds bother you? Do you go to church? If so, do you go every week? I had a client who was able to watch her church services over the internet because the crowds bothered her. Is this an option for you? When you go grocery shopping, do you have a problem going when it's busy or do you try to go when it's probably going to be empty? What happens when you're around a lot of people? What about authority figures[23]? Do you have a problem with police officers? Have you had

---

[23] If you have a problem with authority figures, please tell your attorney before your hearing!

problems with supervisors in the past? Are you fighting with your family more?

The final thing Social Security always asks about is your activities of daily living. They mean your household chores. Are you showering every day? Are you changing clothes? Are you doing laundry? Dishes? Vacuuming? Yard work? Grocery shopping? Who is taking care of these things? If you are not able to handle these activities at home, you probably can't handle a job. This is not to say that you shouldn't do what you can at home. Social Security is probably not going to believe you if your activities aren't close to what you should be able to considering your medical conditions. What you should be doing is paying attention to what your day is like. If you're vacuuming, make a note of how often you're doing it and how long it takes you. I often have people tell me that they do a chore and when I ask them the last time they did it, it turns out that it's been several months. You have a medical impairment. Social Security isn't judging you for what you can and can't do, they're just trying to figure out what you're capable of doing.

You don't need to have mental impairment to have these limitations. Pain and fatigue are fantastic distracters. You're just not going to be as sharp as you once were if you're in a great deal of pain. Most if not all prescription pain medications are going to have side effects like fatigue and mental fogginess similar to the effect you have when you take a cold medicine. It doesn't mean you're losing your mind. You're in a lot of pain so you're not going to be able to keep your house as clean or cook big meals like you did before. Don't be shy about telling Social Security and your attorney about any problems with attention, concentration, trouble with other people and getting your daily activities done. That's exactly what they want to know.

GRID RULES

What if you're capable of sitting eight hours a day, but you're sixty years old and have only done construction work your entire life? Who is going to hire you? Social Security agrees and takes age and past work into account. Once you turn fifty, it's a whole new system[24].

How does this work? First we look at education. We have four classifications:

- Illiterate or unable to communicate in English – some judges are stricter than others on this. You're definitely going to need a translator or be completely unable to read and write.

- Limited or less – did not graduate high school and does not have a GED but speaks English and can read and write

- High school education or more and does not provide for entry into skilled work – this is basically everyone else. If you have a GED, you

---

[24] It's actually forty-five if you don't speak English, are illiterate and have only done physical work. If you're reading this book, presumably you speak and read English, but if this is for a relative or friend, keep this in mind.

fall into this category. If you have a Ph.D., you also fall into this category. It's a little strange, but almost no one qualifies as having direct entry into skilled work. I don't and I have a law degree.

- High School Education or more and provides direct entry into skilled work — in theory this exists probably for people who had attended trade school and can do a skilled job right out of school. Practically speaking, everyone needs some on the job training so this never gets used.

We next talk about transferability of skills from your past work. Remember, we look back at your past fifteen years of work. What we care about is whether your job would have skills that would transfer to a less physical position.

If you dig ditches all day there's probably not a skill that transfers easily to a sit-down job. But let's say I had a job as a lawyer where I travelled all the time and carried around heavy files. I might have stood or walked most of the day and carried fifty pounds or more around with me. If I hurt myself and couldn't drag all those files around with me I would have to quit that job. However, I would easily be able to do a similar job from my desk without all of the walking and lifting.

In fact, being a lawyer is not great from a disability perspective because I can accommodate most problems. I can take breaks when I want to. I can put my feet up at my desk. Because I work for myself, I can (and will unfortunately) even work from bed if I'm sick. You can cut off both my legs[25] and I can probably still do my job if I can function mentally.

This is what we want to know — is there something about your job that will transfer to a less physical job? You might have done construction work, but did you also do the bidding on a project? Did you do payroll? Any paperwork? If you're a stocker at the grocery store, did you do ordering? What about inventory? It might get annoying but Social Security is going to ask for these

---

[25] Please don't cut my legs off.

details about your job for exactly this reason.

If we find that there are no transferable skills to a desk job, you're over 50, and you did work where you were standing all day, guess what? If we think you can do a desk job you win! It's why older people get disability easier.

If you're 55, and you can't lift over 20 pounds and your previous jobs had you lifting over 50 pounds, you win again!

What about those poor desk workers? What do you get out of it? Once you turn 55, we really start to pay attention to your old jobs. We stop looking at whether you could do other jobs. As of age 55, we're looking at minimal transferability to another job. Once you turn 60, it needs to be a job that you can walk straight into and know how to do the job.

These rules are why people might complain about Social Security Disability without really knowing how it works. Your 55 year-old neighbor might be able to mow the grass and still get disability depending on his condition and past work while your thirty year-old cousin who is much sicker gets denied again and again. It's a different standard.

If you want to check out the grids for yourself, they're found at http://www.ssa.gov/OP_Home/cfr20/404/404-app-p02.htm.

Chapter Three: "How do I apply?" Initial Applications

Now that you know the two main types of Social Security and what we look for, it's time to apply. Remember, you need to have stopped working before you apply. If you're making more than $1130 a month, they're just going to kick your application right back to you without doing a medical evaluation.

There's two main ways to go about applying. Regardless of whether you are applying for SSI or SSDI at this point you are completing the same application. You can apply online at http://ssa.gov. Go to the tab marked "Benefits". There is a section called "Apply" and underneath it says "Apply Online for Disability". Alternatively, you can type "Apply for Social Security Disability" into your favorite search engine.

You will then see a blue button that says "Apply for Disability". Click this and begin your application. After completing a few pages you will get a reentry number. *Either print this out or write this down.* If you get kicked out of the online program or need to finish later, this number gets you back in to complete your application.

The biggest mistake I see is when people apply online is that they will finish only half of the application. It will tell you that you have submitted your application, but **unless you have submitted information about your doctors and medications you are not done!** The application isn't that difficult, but make sure that you have done it correctly and finished all parts of the application. If you don't finish all parts of the application, Social Security won't process your case. This is why I sometimes have people tell me that they filled out the application online and then never heard anything.

If you haven't filled out everything correctly, the application won't let you continue on to the next portion of the application so look for the red exclamation points because that means you have made an error.

Print out any summaries that the program gives you. At the end of the application you will receive another number. With this number you can check the status of your application online. You will then get to a page that gives you access to a cover sheet for Social Security and medical authorization forms (SSA-827[26]). Sign these forms and send them in to Social Security.

If you helped someone apply and he was not with you,

---

[26] These forms are found easily by inputting SSA-827 into your search engine as well. SSA will need copies of these every time you submit an appeal so don't stress if you accidentally click past this page. You do not need two witnesses but they do like multiple copies so send at least three.

Social Security will send the application to the claimant to sign. They will not do anything until that application is signed. Make sure it's signed and gets back to Social Security! I would call in about three weeks and make sure they got it.

If you need to apply for SSI, you have two options. The local office needs to get the information from you for the SSI application. You can wait for your local office to contact you, or you can call them yourself. If it's been more than two weeks and you haven't received a call or a letter, give them a call.

The other easy way to apply is to call your local Social Security office and make an appointment to do the application with them. They are busy so this should be reserved for times when you cannot figure out the online application or if the online application won't let you apply.

A tip from a professional though – do NOT call the Social Security national 1800 number for this. CALL YOUR LOCAL OFFICE[27]. The national number is 1-800-772-1213 and it is listed for almost every local office. You can find your local office by going to the Social Security website at http://www.ssa.gov, clicking on "Contact Us", clicking on "Find an Office" and putting in your zip code. It will ask if you need card services and you do not. You can also search for "Social Security find an office" in your favorite search engine. It will give you the national 800 number. You can call this number to get your local office telephone number if you cannot find it on the internet. Otherwise do not call the national 800 number. There is very little that they will be able to help you with and their hold times are very long. Your local office is far more useful for any situation you can think of.

_____

[27]Seriously. I call the 1-800 number a couple times a decade.

When talking to Social Security, always be very polite[28]. It's just easier to get things done and you are asking them for benefits. Tell them you want to apply for Social Security disability and they will make an appointment either on the phone or in the office to do the application. They will help you apply for both SSI and SSDI. Remember if you're not sure which you should be applying for they will tell you.

If you plan on using an attorney and you know the attorney you want to use, contact your attorney and ask if they help you apply. Some offices do and some don't. Some attorneys want you to be denied before they take on your case. It just depends on the attorney. It doesn't mean anything about the attorney and whether they're good or bad. It's just how they choose to handle things. If your attorney helps you apply, it will be an online application. _____

[28] Actually, this is a good idea when dealing with any government agency.

What do I need to have ready to apply?

Social Security needs *a lot* of information when you apply for disability benefits. You need to have it ready. Here is a list.

- Birthdate

- Social Security number

- Birthplace

- If born outside the US, name of birth country and permanent resident card number

- For any marriage that lasted more than ten years or resulted in the death of a spouse

    - Place of marriage and divorce

    - Birthday and social security number of spouse

- Name and date of birth of any children under 18 or under the age of 22 if disabled

- If you had military services the type of duty and branch and service dates

- Employer details for last year and this year including employer name, start and end date and total earnings

- Self-Employment details for this year and the prior two years

- Direct Deposit information if available

- Name and address of a third party contact[29]

- Information about doctors and hospitals

    - Dates first seen and last seen

    - Why did you go?

    - What did they do?

    - If it's a hospital, how long did you stay?

- Medications (current)

- Tests

- Work History – the last fifteen years

- Education and training

- Anyone else who might have records – workers' compensation, prison, public welfare, etc.

---

[29] This is a friend or family member that Social Security can contact who knows about your condition. This is not your doctor or your lawyer. We'll cover this more when we talk about Social Security forms

It's a lot of information but you'll be surprised how much of it is off the top of your head. The reason we want your doctors' information is so that we can get medical records. Most doctors and hospitals can be easily found with a search engine. Just make sure that Social Security and your attorney have the correct location. If you can't remember exactly when you saw a doctor, it's fine to say "March 2012" or even "Spring 2012". What we really want to know is when to request medical records from. If you're not sure, go with an earlier date rather than a later date.

It's the same thing with testing. We don't need to know exactly when you had the MRI on your back or what they found but we do need to know who sent you for it and about when it occurred so we know where to look. If you have blood testing every month you don't have to list every time. Just tell us in the section about the doctor that he sends you for blood tests monthly. We want to know what to look for in your medical records so we know if something important is missing.

Medications should be current medications. I don't need you to put in medications that you had five months ago. That will be in your medical records.

Doctors and hospitals should be listed about a year back from when you stopped working or from your date of disability. I know you might have had some major problems before that. The issue is that you were still working and you are not claiming disability before that. If you had a really important surgery or report, we can still submit that to Social Security. They just don't want to request records going back ten years. I'm not going to do it either. Social Security doesn't care. More importantly, except for the military, most states only require doctors to keep their records for seven years[30].

---

[30] Yet another reason it's a good idea to keep copies of important medical records.

You can tell me how your disability started when you were a kid, but you need to tell that to your doctor and have him relate that to your current problems.

Be thorough when it comes to doctors. Remember - I want anything that's going to limit your ability to work. That said, there are some things I don't care about. I don't want your dentist. Unless your feminine problems limit your work, I don't need your well-woman visit. If you have glasses and your prescription hasn't changed in twenty years, I don't really need that either.

I do want therapists and counselors, home health providers, physical therapists and chiropractors. They provide important medical services, please list them. I also want primary care physicians. They prescribe medications and do referrals. If you've seen your primary care for those reasons, I want them included. If you're not sure if you should include a medical provider, please include them.

Please include any hospitalizations. I get really annoyed when I first hear about a hospitalization in court. Always include an emergency room visit even if you didn't go for a reason that you're claiming disability.

Medications should include over the counter medications. People often don't include them which means we miss out on pills taken for allergies or for high cholesterol like fish oil. Some claimants go to homeopaths which means all their pills are herbal supplements. It's not just prescription medications. Include everything. Nebulizers, inhalers, creams, eye drops and patches also count as medications. If you're not sure, list it.

WHAT HAPPENS NEXT?

First, let's make sure you did everything.

- Did you answer questions about your doctors and medications?

- Did you sign Social Security's medical authorization forms?

- If you planned on applying for SSI benefits, did you answer questions about your finances to SSA or your lawyer?

If the answer to all of these is correct, congratulations! You made it! You filed your application! I've had more people than I can count call me after they got tripped up on the process so stand proud. It's more complicated than it seems.

Next the application goes from Social Security to the local Disability Determination Services. This office is actually run by the state you live in. It will take some time for the case to get processed there. It can be anywhere from a few weeks to a couple of months.

Sometimes a state will get overloaded with applications. When this happens there's a couple of clearing houses they go to. There's one in Oklahoma and one in Arkansas. It's fine. It doesn't mean there's anything wrong with your case. It's not good, it's not bad. It means your state has a lot of applications and there's some overflow. They may not move any faster or any slower on your application. The only difference is that if they need to contact you, there may be a time zone effect in place.

After you get transferred to Disability Determination Services (DDS), your case then gets assigned to an examiner. At this time they request your medical records and also send you some forms.

If you have medical records to send in, this is when you want to send in your medical records. If you send them in before, they may get lost at Social Security or DDS. On the forms there is usually an examiner with a phone number and extension. Call that person, say that you have medical records and they will send you a fax cover sheet with a bar code to fax them in. It then goes into your electronic file. *You do not have to submit all of your medical records.* They will request your records and they're pretty good about getting them. If there's a report you really want considered or your doctor has written a letter, this is where and when you submit it.

You will receive forms in the mail. Everyone gets the same forms. It's called a Function Report and it asks about your daily activities. Because they try to cover all impairments there are going to be some parts of the report that just won't apply to you. Don't worry about it. They ask about what a normal day looks like for you. Whether you take care of any children or pets, whether you do any chores, how you take care of yourself, whether you drive, can you cook, can you go out alone, can you handle money, can you concentrate, how far can you walk, does your medication have side effects? Coincidentally, these are the same things I've been telling you to pay attention to.

Again, I know that it's really hard to know how long you can do these things. Just do your best. Include what you can do on an average day but also include your worst day. This is not the time to be proud and tell them that you can do anything. If you can't lift a gallon of milk, say so. It needs to be consistent with your medical records. Don't get paranoid, just tell the truth. Some days are going to be harder than others. Some things you aren't going to have any problems with. It doesn't mean anything for your case.

The friend or family member that you put down on your application as the third party contact is also going to get this form. You don't need to work on them together and they don't need to say the exact same thing. Each of you just needs to tell the truth.

You will also get a Work History Report asking for information about the jobs you held for the last fifteen years. If you did the same job for more than one employer, you can lump them together. They're more interested in the kind of work you did, not the employer.

If you did a job less than two months you don't need to include it on the form. You will need to estimate how much time you spent walking, standing, sitting, crouch, squatting, reaching, handling, etc. Just do your best. They mostly care about standing, sitting and walking so try to make those equal to eight hours.

The form also asks about how much you lifted. I win a lot of cases on this information so try to be accurate. Think about how much you lifted regularly and how much you were required to lift on the job. Often jobs will have a minimum lifting requirement. You need to include that.

The forms say they need to be back within ten days but often you won't receive them for five or six days. It's fine to call DDS and ask for an extension. I've never had a request for an extension on forms turned down. They want them quickly, but an extra few days is fine. Be polite and ask for the extension though. Please do not annoy your DDS examiner. Leave a message if no one answers.

Once they have your forms, things become very quiet. Things are happening on your case - they just don't need any input from you. DDS is getting your medical records and they're passing them to the in-house doctor who looks at them. It takes a long time to get the medical records and they have a lot of cases.

Here's the question – should you be updating them with your medical status? Probably not. If you're just going to the doctor and things aren't changing much they don't need to know. It will just slow down your case and not make a difference. New medications, new x-rays, even a new MRI probably isn't a reason to call DDS. However, a major hospitalization, a major surgery like a knee replacement, spinal surgery[31] or brain surgery will qualify

---

[31] Not an epidural, nerve ablation or probably even a spinal stimulator. Actual spinal surgery where they cut you open and operate on your disks.

as something you should tell DDS about because it will likely affect your case for longer than twelve months.

Unless DDS needs information from you, just sit back and relax. If you're really going nuts wanting to know what's going on with your case, call the main DDS number on your form and ask for status. They'll tell you if it's still pending. During the medical records gathering stage, there's not much to do.

If you want to contribute, this is the time you can gather reports from your doctors saying what you can and cannot do. You can keep diaries tracking your pain and good and bad days. If you're having migraines or seizures keep track of those as well. Diabetics can keep track of their blood sugar.

DDS may ask you for additional information. They may send out questionnaires about headaches, seizures and drugs and alcohol. Like before, be as honest as possible.

They're just trying to gather as much information as they can before they turn the information over to the in-house doctor to make a decision.

CONSULTATIVE EXAMS

If the in-house doctor decides there is not enough information in the medical record, DDS decides to send you for a medical exam. This happens in almost every case, so do not be surprised. It doesn't mean they didn't get your medical records or that they didn't look at them. It also doesn't mean that they plan on denying your case.

The physical exams generally last about ten to fifteen minutes. You will be expected to walk, bend, get on and off the exam table, perform some simple maneuvers and that's about it. The doctor may or may not touch you. The doctor may or may not know what your diagnosis is or have seen any of your medical records. Put forth your best effort to do what you can. Tell the doctor what your diagnoses are and why you feel you can't work. Be specific. Do not just say "Because I'm in pain." *List actual diagnoses.* The consultative exam notice will say whether you should bring any medical records or not. The doctor will almost definitely not have any time to review records or x-rays that you bring.

Sometimes the consultative exam will include x-rays. The x-rays may not be for the condition that you think is most serious. This does not mean they didn't read your file. It means they need more information because they don't have enough information about the body part they're x-raying.

Usually my clients leave these exams feeling very frustrated. The exams are very short and sometimes the doctors do not seem very interested. The doctors are given instructions by DDS and are generally not asked to review any medical records. They are not paid very well for the exams so they try to do as many exams as possible in a day.

I cannot tell you how to win your case based on these exams, but I can give you some tips. When the doctor asks why you can't work please be specific. Don't just say "Because of my pain." Give actual diagnoses. The doctor hasn't seen your medical records and information from DDS may or may not be correct. Say for example "Because of my diabetes and the herniated discs in my lower back." It gives the doctor much more specific things to look at. If you mention pain and nothing else, the doctor doesn't know what to look for in his exam. Don't just say, "Because I'm so tired." Everyone's tired. The doctor is likely tired. That isn't going to be enough. You might have migraines and your physical exam will look normal. Remember to include as many diagnoses as you can remember.

The doctor is going to be watching you get up and down from the examination table and how you move. Almost everything the doctor will have you do will be assuming you have a back injury. Don't worry about it, but that's why it's important to tell the doctor what your medical conditions are so he knows what to look for. The doctor will ask you to walk, squat, bend, etc. Try to do everything he asks. If you really can't do what he is asking – don't. Please don't hurt yourself. But don't exaggerate your pain either. You really don't want the doctor to write down that he thinks you're faking in your file. If you have had surgery, or undergone treatment for your condition beyond medication, let the doctor know.

DDS may also send you for mental exams. The mental exams are longer than the physical exams and usually last about an hour. You will discuss your psychological history including any abuse you may have suffered. There will be extensive questions about substance abuse.

Please tell the truth. Inconsistent information about substance abuse is far more harmful than the substance abuse itself assuming it's in the past[32]. The psychologist will administer a mini mental status exam where you are checked for any mental deficits. Feel free to discuss any stressors in your life at this time. It's perfectly fine to say that you are having trouble coping because of your condition. DDS is really looking to see what trouble you're having with attention and concentration so be sure to mention if you're having trouble in those areas. Also mention if you're having trouble getting along with people and getting things done. My clients tend to be less frustrated with these exams possibly because the examiners take longer with them.

There are two opinions on whether you need to go to these exams. Some attorneys will tell you that you don't need to go and that the information in your medical

---

[32] See Chapter Eleven on substance abuse.

record is enough and to get additional reports from your doctor. I am not here to tell you not to follow your attorney's advice. Please follow your attorney's advice! Your attorney knows what DDS is going to accept instead of an exam and when to just go to an exam. This is not a game you want to play on your own. Some of this depends on the DDS office the attorney is dealing with.

The problem with not going to an exam without the participation of an attorney is that you will definitely be denied for not cooperating with DDS. It doesn't matter how strong your case is. When and if you end up in front of a judge, you will have to explain why you didn't feel like you had to go to the exams that DDS requested. This never goes well. Go to the exam.

There are some reasons for not going to the exam or asking them to reschedule:

- You are in the hospital.

- You moved to another state and you previously told them you moved to another state.

- They scheduled another exam at exactly the same time or so close as to make it impossible to get to the second exam. (This has happened.)

- You are so incapacitated that you cannot physically leave the house. I do not mean a cold. I do not mean you do not feel like going. I do not mean you are sick or in pain because that's probably always the case. I mean you cannot physically leave the house because you are trapped under something heavy or you are getting home health services and are under doctor's orders not to leave the house.

- You are dead.

Fun Fact - The doctor and/or administrative staff will often be watching you in the parking lot and waiting room. This information is then included in the report. Just be aware.

Even if the doctor tells you that he believes you are disabled you still may not win your case. I've had lots of clients who swear the doctor told them he was going to write a good report who then were denied. There is another doctor at DDS who does the final evaluation on your case who may decide you aren't disabled.

Even if you have no mental disability, you will likely be sent for a mental exam. This is because you at some point hinted in your medical records that you were unhappy because you can't work and you're in pain or that you had trouble concentrating. It's not a bad thing to go to the mental exam even if you don't have a mental disability. The worst thing that happens is they say that you have no mental limitations and you're in the same position you were before. But often we can get some additional limitations in concentration or attention in the record and it can be very helpful to the case.

If your disability is primarily mental, they're less likely to send you to a physical exam, but they may do so as well.

Again, any additional limitations are useful, so go to the exam.

If I can stress anything about these exams, it's to tell the truth. Try to do what the doctors ask you to do to the best of your ability without hurting yourself.

Once DDS has the report from the consultative exam, the DDS doctor makes a determination. You will get the decision about a month later. It takes about six to eight months to get a decision from Social Security on an Initial Application. If you need status on your case, you can always call Social Security or DDS and ask what is going on. You can also use your reentry number and check online at https://secure.ssa.gov/apps6z/IAPS/applicationStatus. This will really only tell you if your case has been closed or not, but it's still good to know if you need to file an appeal in case you're worried you didn't get the denial letter.

Denials

If you were denied, the letter will be titled "Social Security Notice" and tell you that you are not disabled under their rules. It will list the medical records they used to decide the claim. This may or may not be a complete list so don't panic when you receive the letter. Social Security will then tell you whether they think you can return to your old job or if you can do some other work.

The only really important things on the letter are the date on the letter and that you were denied on a medical basis versus a financial basis. You have sixty days to appeal the decision with an additional five days for mailing. The fact that they denied you on a medical basis is important because if Social Security denied you because you make too much money or you don't have enough quarters of coverage, we need to handle the case differently[33]. As long as they think you can do some sort of work, we can continue on with a regular appeal.

If you were approved, congratulations! Skip ahead to the chapter on how awards work.

[33] See Chapter One and the discussion on SSI and SSDI.

Chapter Four: "I have to do this again?" Requests for Reconsideration and Hearings

The next stage is the Request for Reconsideration. Basically it's the exact same process as before, but someone new looks at your case. It takes a little less time, but yes, it goes through Disability Determination Services again.

Before starting the appeals process, you might be wondering if you should even appeal your case. The short answer is yes. Of course you should. If you take nothing else away from this book, take this away. *Almost everyone is denied.* It has very little to do with the merits of the case. The denial rate at the Initial Application level is about 70%[34]. You shouldn't feel bad you were denied, nor should you assume you won't get through eventually. The trick to Social Security is perseverance.

The only reason you shouldn't appeal is if you recovered from your illness, you're ready to go back to work and you have absolutely no chance of going back out of work. Even then, I might suggest appealing just in case you have trouble working and you end up off work again. You can always withdraw your case later[35].

Now for the bad news. Requests for Reconsiderations have a 90% denial rate. Yes, you read that right. If the denial rate is that high, then it doesn't really seem like a good use of anyone's time. Why bother then? In fact, some states don't.

Nine states and part of another skip the Reconsideration stage entirely. When you file an appeal in these states,

---

[34] http://www.ssa.gov/policy/docs/statcomps/di_asr/2011/sect04.html

[35] See Chapter Eight on trial work attempts.

you go directly to a hearing with an Administrative Law Judge. These states are:[36]

- Alabama

- Alaska

- California (Los Angeles North and West branches only[37])

- Colorado

- Louisiana

- Michigan

- Missouri

- New Hampshire

- New York

- Pennsylvania

Other states may be added as time goes by. If you think you filed for a Reconsideration and suddenly you're

---

[36] https://secure.ssa.gov/poms.nsf/lnx/0412015100

[37] Don't stress. When you file online or with SSA, they'll automatically send it to a hearing if you're in the district that goes directly to a hearing.

waiting for a hearing - you may be in a state that skips Reconsiderations.

FILING YOUR APPEAL

The easiest (and preferred) way to file your appeal is online. You will do the exact same thing to file both your Request for Reconsideration and your Hearing Request. Go again to the Social Security website at http://www.ssa.gov. Find the tab that says Benefits. There will be a menu that says Apply. Underneath it will be a selection for Appeal a Decision. Please select Appeal a Decision. You can also just type "Appeal a Social Security Disability Decision" into your favorite search engine.

Click on the blue button that says "Appeal Our Recent Medical Decision". This will take you through the Reconsideration online. You need to have the date from your denial letter. If you're off by a day or two it will still let you complete the application.

Like the online application, there are two parts to the online appeal. You will complete a section with your name and address and why you are appealing your decision. Then there is a section with your medical information. You need to complete both parts or you did not complete all of it! If it did not ask you about your doctors and medication you did not complete your appeal.

The appeal will ask you why you are appealing. Just say "There is an error in both law and fact. I cannot work." You will get a reentry number. Print it out or write it down in case the program has a problem or you need to finish later.

Once you get to the second part of the appeal it will ask whether you have any new conditions or limitations.

They want to know if you have developed any new problems since you filed your Initial Application or last appeal. Try to think of something to put in here even if your condition hasn't changed much. If you say nothing has changed, your case will not be considered as closely. Even though there's a 90% denial rate at the Reconsideration level, you still want someone to review your case properly.

They also ask about your daily activities and ability to care for your personal needs. This is your chance to talk about how long you can sit, stand, and walk and how much you can lift. Also talk about attention and concentration. Focus on fatigue and your really bad days. Be specific. This is not the time to say, "I have pain." Or "I get tired sometimes." We all have pain and get tired. Why is it that you can't go to work? Why is your pain and fatigue worse than the normal person's?

As before, list all of your doctors that you've seen since your Initial Application or last appeal. If you can't remember exact dates, give enough information so that Social Security knows what medical records to request.

The appeal software can be difficult so if you are more than 60 days after your appeal or if it just won't let you complete the appeal online, you have some options. Call your local office and complete the appeal with them. They may have answers why the appeal software won't work.

You can also send in a paper appeal, but you run the risk that it may get lost at Social Security. If you decide to go the paper appeal route, I suggest going to Social Security yourself and bringing it in person so that you get a receipt. The paper Request for Reconsideration is found at http://www.socialsecurity.gov/forms/ssa-561.pdf. The paper Hearing Request is at http://www.socialsecurity.gov/forms/ha-501.pdf. You will also need to complete a Disability Report with your medical information. This is found at http://www.socialsecurity.gov/forms/ssa-3441.pdf.

No matter whether you do the appeal online or in paper form you will need to send in Social Security's medical authorization forms again. They need three copies. Find someone to witness them. If you complete the form online they will direct you to print them out. The forms can be found at http://www.socialsecurity.gov/forms/ssa-827.pdf.

If you are past the sixty day appeal rate, you need to ask for Social Security to accept your appeal for good cause. I might call Social Security and let them know why you didn't file your appeal on time. Was the denial not mailed to you? Did you move? If it's more than a day or two you're going to need something better than "I forgot". If it's longer than a month and you don't have a really, really good excuse you'll likely need to start over.

This is why you really don't want to ignore any mail from Social Security[38].

At this point, your case will be sent off to Disability Determination Services to go through the process again. It takes a bit less time than before. You should expect to get an answer in about four to six months.

You will get the same forms in the mail to fill out. Please do not just copy your forms from before. Social Security is looking to see if anything has changed in your condition. Also, you didn't get through before, so putting the same information down on your Function Report is not likely to get you disability this time. If they send you another Work History report and you haven't tried working since your first application, you can copy your previous Work History report.

---

[38] It's also why some people prefer to have an attorney. The attorney gets the same mail and you're less likely to miss deadlines. If this all sounds too complicated you might be better off with an attorney.

If for some reason they didn't send you to a consultative exam before, they will probably send you to one now. They usually send you to two physical exams and two mental exams over the course of your disability case. Again, tell the truth and be sure to mention any new conditions that have popped up since your last appointment. DDS will not be sending you to the same doctor as before.

Remember, there is a 90% denial rate at the Reconsideration level, so do not expect to get through. The statistics are just against you. No one should have their feelings hurt when a denial letter comes in the mail. I know it's very frustrating, but it doesn't mean that you won't eventually be found disabled. It's just a stage you have to go through in order to get in front of a judge.

Once you get your denial, go ahead and do the appeal the exact same way you did it for the Request for Reconsideration. Once the local Social Security office has your Hearing Request, they will transfer your case to the local Office of Disability Adjudication and Review. Then the real fun begins.

Chapter Five: "Why do I have to go to court?" Social Security Hearings

All over the country we have Offices of Disability Adjudication and Review just waiting to hear your case and determine your disability. There are 168 of them with almost 1,400 administrative law judges[39]. These are federal administrative courts and they are official court houses but less formal so cases can move through the system faster.

We don't have the formal rules of evidence that you see on television. The judges let every bit of evidence in. I very rarely get to stand up and shout "Objection!" (Although it's really fun when I do.)

---

[39] http://www.ssa.gov/appeals/ho_locator.html

Most importantly there's no opposing counsel. This means that unlike on television, there's no attorney on the other side trying to prove you're not disabled. It's up to you and your attorney to prove your case.

Once your case gets transferred to the Office of Disability Adjudication and Review (ODAR), you'll get a letter saying that it's there and which office is handling your case. The letter is slightly misleading because it says you will receive notice of your hearing twenty days before your hearing. An awful lot of people read this as meaning they have a hearing in twenty days. You do not.

In reality, you'll get a hearing notice a couple of months before your hearing. They're required by law to give you twenty days notice. If you have an attorney, the hearing office will call the attorney to schedule the hearing so you'll have extra notice. If you don't have an attorney, they won't call you to schedule the hearing.

While you're waiting for the hearing, you might get a cd in the mail with the exhibit file on it including all of your medical records. Take a look at the cd as soon as possible to see what's missing. You can also call the hearing office[40] and request a copy of the cd. Once your case is at the hearing office, they stop requesting your medical records. If you don't have an attorney, you're going to have to get your records and get them into the hearing office.

When you get the cd, they will also give you a fax cover sheet with a bar code on it. You can fax the medical records to the hearing office and it will go directly into the electronic file. You can also just mail them into the hearing office. If you do have an attorney, it's very important at this point to keep your attorney updated on all your doctor's appointments. Your attorney can upload

---

[40] The phone number is online and on the letter you just received.

your records directly online and check to make sure they were received.

Depending on where you are, the hearing wait time can vary. Some places are around six months, other offices can be up to two years. The internet has current waiting times for hearing offices at http://www.ssa.gov/appeals/DataSets/05_Average_Proces sing_Time_Report.pdf.

Social Security knows that people waiting for a hearing generally do not have much money and cannot travel far. Therefore, if you are not close to a hearing office, they will do video teleconference hearings in local Social Security offices. The judges used to travel to the remote hearing offices but it got too expensive. If you have to travel more than 75 miles each way, Social Security will pay you mileage and some expenses if you get them pre-approved. Mileage does not have to be pre-approved.

Do you need an attorney?

Because I'm a Social Security attorney, my opinion is biased, but hear me out anyway. When people are about to go in front of a judge they start thinking about lawyers. Lots of people get benefits without an attorney and it's a reasonable question to ask if you need one. Do you have to get an attorney? Of course not! There are lots of different factors that go into a case. You may have a great case and you may have an easy judge. If you think you can handle it yourself that might be why you're reading this book in the first place. The country is a big place, so you're likely not in the right location to hire me anyway, but I like people to make an informed decision.

First, let's talk about attorney's fees and how they work for Social Security. No one applying for Social Security disability benefits feels like they have money to spare so we plan ahead. Our fees are set by the government so all attorneys *should* be charging the same.

Fees are set based on your back pay from Social Security. Once you're approved, you get paid back all the money you should have been getting from Social Security but weren't because you hadn't been approved yet. We get paid out of the back pay for Social Security. The fees are 25% of the back pay but not more than $6000.00. If you get $10,000.00 worth of back pay, the attorney gets $2,500.00. If you get $50,000.00 worth of back pay, the attorney only gets $6,000.00. Got it?

There are some variables. If the attorney has to take your case past a hearing to the Appeals Council and Federal Court, many attorneys charge a straight 25% and that's legal. Some attorneys charge for medical records since doctors and hospitals charge us for medical records. There should be nothing up front. I've heard of a few attorneys asking for one to two hundred dollars up front for medical records. Others charge for the records as they go. Often attorneys ask for the cost of medical records at the end of the case. Otherwise you should not be paying any money to your attorney. Beyond those variables, the fees should be the same. Consultations should be free.

Every once in a great while, we have to do work on an hourly basis if back pay isn't available. These are usually overpayment cases or if your Social Security has been cut off. Your attorney will explain these to you. Social Security still has to approve these fees.

If an attorney wants more than 25% of your back pay, or more than $6,000.00 of your back pay at the hearing level or lower, you have a problem. Again, our fees are set by Social Security and they are approved by Social Security. We can't get paid until Social Security approves the fee.

- *Never, ever sign a fee agreement with an attorney if you don't understand what you are signing.*

- *Never, ever pay any attorney money without signing a fee agreement.*

I don't care if it's a Social Security case or not. You need to understand it or don't sign it.

But why get an attorney at all? Even if your attorney does absolutely nothing and sits there like a potted plant, there is some benefit to having an attorney on the record.

First, no one wants to go in front of a judge alone. I'm an attorney and I wouldn't want to go in front of a judge alone for anything more than a traffic ticket. An attorney can tell you what to expect, what the judge is like, submit records, check the file to make sure the records are up to date, and check for the decision after the hearing. It's nice to have a friend in the courtroom.

Second, there's something called a rocket docket. When a claimant doesn't have an attorney, often they don't show up for hearings[41]. Some (not all or even most) judges are known to schedule seven or eight cases at the same time or very close together assuming most of them won't show up and the ones that do show up get ten minute hearings. I'm not saying this to scare you. But simply by having an attorney - any attorney – listed, you automatically get a full hearing and your case gets a more detailed consideration. When I have people come to me after they had a hearing that they went to alone, I always ask how long the hearing was. Sometimes they really were ten minute hearings. It's not fair, but it's something to consider.

Of course, if you have a good attorney it's much more helpful. The attorney will know how to evaluate your case, what legal arguments to make, what records and reports to get from your doctors, how to cross-examine the experts, how to deal with that specific judge and how

---

[41] It's often because they moved and the person has no idea a hearing is taking place. I'm not implying anything shady is going on.

to prepare you for your case.

In many cases there are the makings of a winnable case already sitting in the file if someone just looked properly at the case. Most[42] Social Security attorneys work with the same judges and experts for years and know which arguments work and which don't. They can prepare you for the questions the judge will ask, what to wear and how to behave.

The attorney can also explain what's happening in court and what happened after the hearing is over. It seems like every time I leave court my client says, "What just happened?" Familiarity with the judges is very helpful. Some judges are grouchy and yell a lot but approve most claimants. Some judges smile and are friendly to everyone and deny almost everyone. Your attorney can

---

[42] Some attorneys travel all over the country for hearings which makes things a bit more difficult. They're better at handling new judges and unexpected experts though.

give you a better idea of what just happened than anyone else.

Plus, if you need to appeal the case, the attorney will make sure that everything was done to make sure you have the best possible case to appeal.

However, I will agree that in some cases there just isn't that much for an attorney to do in the actual courtroom. Sometimes I do go in and answer a few questions about the file. Then the judge asks the claimant a few questions and that's it. The trouble is I never know which of those cases it's going to be. Some cases I expect to be easy I spend an hour and a half arguing my head off while my client sits there in a daze. That's the problem, you don't know.

Finally, there's the question of when to get an attorney. Some attorneys won't take cases until the hearing level while others want them before you file the first application. Others will help you apply while some won't. You might decide that you want to see if you get approved at the initial application level before you hire an attorney. Or you decide you don't want to do any of it on your own. It's your choice.

If you're going to find an attorney, I'd first ask my family and friends if they have used anyone they really liked. There are positives and negatives to using the big firms versus the small local firms. The big firms are a clearing house and they get the job done. You likely won't talk to an attorney until you're at a hearing, but they're effective. The smaller local firms will have more personal contact, and probably allow you to talk to attorneys more. There may be more variance in quality so you'll want a good recommendation. Look at experience.

The most important thing is to find a firm you're comfortable with. You're not paying them by the hour so find a firm that you feel comfortable calling with questions without feeling like you are bothering them. Do they answer your questions? Are they friendly? Do you feel like they care about your case? Do they return phone calls? Do you understand where your case is at? Do they give you reasonable expectations of what to expect? It's fine to call more than one firm and see who you like best.

You hold the power in the attorney-client relationship. If you ever decide that you don't want to use the firm anymore, call the firm and tell them that you don't want to use them anymore and ask for a withdrawal letter. They're required to withdraw and give you a copy of your file.

HOW TO PREPARE FOR YOUR HEARING

You will get notice of your hearing at least twenty days before your hearing but likely much longer. If you cannot go, call the hearing office and let them know.

Please have a good reason. If it's the day of the hearing and you can't go and don't give them a good reason why, otherwise your case might be dismissed.

Try to get another copy of your cd if you haven't received one recently to make sure all of your medical records are on there. If you have an attorney, make sure they have all your medical records. Remember, your attorney isn't psychic. If you don't tell anyone about a doctor or hospital, it won't be in your file. Obvious I know, but you'd be surprised how often it comes up.

If you have an attorney, he will schedule a hearing preparation with you shortly before the hearing. This is so the two of you can go over everything the hearing will entail: how the hearing works, what you should wear, how long it will last, and the questions the judge will ask. If your attorney hasn't scheduled this with you, it's okay to ask for one. You need to know what to expect before facing the judge.

Please follow all of your attorney's advice regarding your hearing. Your attorney knows what works for your particular judge and hearing office. I am just giving some general information.

Clothing for your hearing should be casual. Do not dress in a suit or anything professional. You will look like you're going to a job interview and that implies that you are able to work. No one likes to lose a case based on clothing. I've heard advice like women should not have their nails painted or do their makeup or do their hair. I don't think it needs to go quite that far. Wear what you might wear to a doctor's office. You don't have to show up looking as pathetic as you possibly can. The judge will see through that. Just look like yourself.

Also, please no short shorts, no tank tops, no t-shirts with anything written on it, no hats, and no bandannas. You never know if your favorite sports team is the one team the judge absolutely hates. Don't wear a t-shirt with anything funny or it might look like you are not taking the hearing seriously. This is why I say just a plain shirt. Remain neutral. I live in Arizona and it gets really hot in the summer but cover yourself up anyway. Wear clothes that hide your tattoos as best you can. Take out any piercings that are not in your earlobes if you can. Jewelry should be at a minimum because the judges like to think they're giving money to the needy. I understand that a good percentage of people applying for disability have trouble putting on normal shoes so if you have to do sandals or flip flops or even slippers, do what you have to do.

If you normally use a cane, crutches, walker or wheelchair, bring it. There's usually a bit of walking from the parking lot to the hearing office. The hearing offices always have handicapped parking available and have elevators and ramps. But sometimes there's a bit of walking to actually get to the hearing room. Bring whatever you would normally bring in that situation. There's also usually quite a bit of waiting and sitting. If you would normally bring a pillow or something to help you sit, bring that. However, do not bring a walker or wheelchair if you would normally not bring one. It's not a bad idea to check out where the hearing office is in advance and ask your attorney how much walking there will be. The Tucson hearing office used to have parking a block or so away from the office and part of it was uphill. It's moved now, but it was an awful lot of walking for a disabled person.

Take your normal medications unless they would make you fall asleep or make you unable to answer questions. The judge needs to see you on a normal day. However, we still need to you function.

People always want to know if they should look the judge up on the internet. Be careful. It's a natural reaction and there is quite a bit of information on the internet about each judge. Here's the problem though. If the judge has a high approval rate, the claimant goes in very cocky and the hearing goes badly. If the judge has a bad approval rate, the claimant goes in very defensively thinking they're going to lose and it goes badly.

Plus there's just a lot of bad information. I had a claimant call me assuming she was going to lose because there was bad information on the internet about a judge. Someone had posted that he had epilepsy and was in a wheelchair and how could this judge deny him? Now as it happens this is a great judge and my client had a great case.

I pointed out that just because someone is in a wheelchair it doesn't mean he can't work. All of the working disabled people in wheelchairs might get a little irritated by that notion. We don't know how often that guy had seizures either. He could have one seizure a year. The judge may have been completely correct to deny him. A person having seizures in a wheelchair sounds terrible but in actuality the person may not have been disabled at all by Social Security standards. The internet can be a very misleading place. I have found that everyone does much better if the claimants go into the hearing just thinking of the judge as a person and not as a percentage.

That said, I do prepare my clients what to expect from a judge in terms of temperament. I warn my clients if the judge moves extremely fast or yells at everyone or is easy going. I want my clients to know what to expect in that regard. If the judge yells at everyone who enters the courtroom then my client needs to be prepared.

Look at your cd if you don't have an attorney. See what's in your medical records. If your doctors are saying that you're not following doctor's orders or are faking your illnesses it's best to know before your hearing.

The day of the hearing

Get to your hearing at least a half an hour to an hour early. Sometimes the hearing before you finishes ahead of schedule and you want to be ready. Your attorney will direct you how early he wants you there. Sometimes you may do your hearing preparation at the hearing office before the hearing. Most of the time it will be a day or two before the hearing.

You and anyone with you will need to be checked by the security guard. The hearing office is a federal court house so check before you go that you don't have anything that could be considered a weapon on you like Swiss army knives, scissors or pepper spray. Please don't joke with the security guards about weapons or bombs. They have to take that seriously. Remember, sometimes people are very angry with the hearing office over their result or have serious mental disorders so the security guard is there to keep you safe, too.

Check-in with the front desk and let them know you're there for your hearing. After that, either wait for your attorney if you have one, or sit and wait for your name to be called. Sometimes hearings run late. This may not be due to the judge. Depending on the situation, some hearings just take a lot longer than others. Don't panic. They won't forget about you.

The front desk will likely give you a disc with your exhibits on it. You will have probably already received one. You can look at it if you like, there are computers available to use or you can bring a laptop. The discs are encrypted. The front desk will give you the code.

You may or may not be allowed an observer. This is something you want to call ahead to the hearing office and ask about. Your attorney will also likely know if you can have an observer. The Judge may decide the day of the hearing that he doesn't want observers in the courtroom. Do not complain.

Your observer is there to observe. Your observer is not there to remind you of things you forgot, correct you if you say something wrong, add in his or her opinion, argue with the Judge, or hand you any items. The observer is not there to testify and should say nothing. If the observer is a distraction or tries to talk, the observer will be told to leave the courtroom.

Generally, you do not bring any witnesses to the hearing with you. Any doctors' opinions you want considered should be submitted in writing. If your friends or family members want to testify on your behalf, they should also write a letter. There are a couple of exceptions where a witness is appropriate:

- If the claimant is a child and cannot testify for himself a parent should come and testify as well. If the child is under thirteen, another adult should be present to take the child out of the courtroom if needed.

- If the claimant is so mentally ill or has had brain damage to the point that the claimant does not understand how bad the disability is you will also need another witness. For example, the claimant says, "I get tired and confused a lot." The parent then comes in and says, "We have to keep the stove unplugged because he forgets and we have fires."

The point of the hearing is so that the Judge can hear from *you* what your disability is and what your life is like. Chances are you've spent the past couple of years wishing someone at Social Security would just listen to you and understand what's going on and how hard everything is for you. This is your chance.

THE HEARING

The hearing monitor will come and get you for your hearing from the waiting room. Hearing monitors are basically the Judge's clerks. They run the hearing recording equipment, they take notes and they make sure everything runs smoothly. If you have an observer, double check with the hearing monitor that the Judge allows observers.

The hearing rooms are federal court rooms but are less formal than you see on television. Because they're administrative court rooms, they're usually smaller. There aren't rows of seats for people to come and watch because they're closed to the public.

The Judge sits on a high bench behind a tall desk. The hearing monitor sits next to him. There is a long conference table in front of the Judge. You will sit in front of the Judge with your attorney, if you have one. Each court room is set up a little different so the hearing monitor will tell you where to sit. There will be a small microphone in front of you. The microphone will not make your voice louder. It is to record the hearing in case of an appeal.

There are two computers sitting on the table. This is for your attorney and the Vocational Expert if you have one. There should also be a box of tissues and a pitcher of water with cups. You can use both if you need to. If the

Judge is not in the room when you enter, you should stand when he does enter. The Judge is always referred to as "Sir" or "Your Honor". Politeness and respect for the Judge will never hurt your case.

During the hearing, you can stand up and stretch if you need to. Remember, most of the cases that the Judge sees are back pain cases. You can even walk a bit just make sure that you're talking near the microphone that is on the table. Before you stand up the first time, please ask the Judge's permission to stand. Do this even if the Judge said you could stand. They're tape recording the hearing and this gets it on the record at what point during the hearing that you needed to stand up. Don't be shy about standing up and stretching either. It doesn't hurt your case to stand up. What does hurt your case is saying you can sit for fifteen minutes and then sitting there for forty-five minutes because you're trying to be polite but really you're in agony. Stand up and stretch when you need to.

You can also go to the bathroom if you need to. Lots of cases have bathroom-related conditions. If you feel a panic attack coming on, please take a break as well and explain what's going on. Crying is also natural. It's why they have tissues on the table. I promise you, the Judge has seen it all and you'll have to make a real effort to surprise the Judge[43].

When it comes to answering questions, you need to speak loudly enough that the Judge can hear you and the hearing monitor can get everything on tape. You need to answer everything out loud. This means that you should not nod your head, but instead answer, "Yes." Don't point to where it hurts, but instead say, "I hurt in my lower back and then it travels down my left leg." The Judge and your attorney will remind you, but try to remember.

---

[43] Please don't try to surprise the Judge.

Answer every question as honestly as you can. If you do not remember, it's far better to say, "I don't remember" then try to guess. Medications and pain are great distracters so chances are memory loss is part of your disability claim.

Most importantly, make sure you understand the question before you answer it even if it's your attorney asking the question. Sometimes the air conditioning or heating is loud. Sometimes we have someone on the phone who is asking questions. Sometimes the judges and the attorneys just do too many hearings and we ask questions in a weird way. The point is if a question doesn't make sense, it's probably not you. It's much, much easier to say, "I'm sorry, can you repeat the question?" then to try to answer what you think we asked and end up saying something you didn't mean to.

Try to keep your answers short and answer only the question that was asked. If you have an attorney, the attorney can come back around and ask all of the questions that weren't asked by the Judge. If the Judge asks if you have a valid driver's license, the Judge really just wants to know if your driver's license was taken away, not how much you drive. Your attorney will come back and ask how much you drive, how far you drive, if you drive at night, if you drive on freeways, can you drive on your medication, do you drive in strange neighborhoods, do you need to have someone with you, etc.

I know you've been waiting years for the hearing and you want to get everything out and you're afraid you won't get to. This is why I always do a hearing preparation before a hearing so I can get all of the information in a more relaxed setting and then during the hearing I can get the important information out for the judge. I really don't like people using notes during a hearing, but if you're doing it alone, you might want to have a list of things to cover if the Judge doesn't. Just don't refer to it throughout the hearing. When the Judge asks if there's anything else, then scan the list and see if you missed anything.

After the hearing, there's always going to be something you forgot or something you wish you would have answered differently. It happens to everyone. Don't beat yourself up about it. Be aware that it's going to happen and try to relax.

VOCATIONAL EXPERTS

There may be experts the Judge chooses to have at the hearing. Usually a Vocational Expert is present. Sometimes the Vocational Expert appears over the telephone. Having a Vocational Expert appear at your hearing is neither a good sign nor a bad sign for your case. A lot of judges have them at all their hearings. It really only means that the judge would like some additional help seeing if there are any jobs you can perform with specific limitations.

To become a Vocational Expert, a person has a graduate degree in vocational counseling, vocational rehabilitation or industrial psychology. Part of their job is surveying different types of jobs and how they are performed in the national economy. They help people find jobs after they have been injured in an accident or have learning difficulties. For example, if you fall off a ladder and hurt your leg so badly that you can't stand all day and paint houses, a vocational expert might help you train to do computer work.

For a Social Security hearing, the Vocational Expert is there to say what jobs are appropriate if you have certain limitations. The judge might say, "Can a person with the claimant's age, experience and background who can sit eight hours a day but cannot use her right hand do any work?" The Vocational Expert would then look at the available jobs in the area and look at what the claimant used to do and see if the claimant could do her old job or if there are any other jobs the claimant might be able to do. A good Vocational Expert might also ask for more information like whether it's her dominant hand or not. Some judges have Vocational Experts in every hearing, some judges never use them.

The Vocational Expert also classifies all jobs according to the Dictionary of Occupational Titles[44]. Every job has a nine digit code and is classified as to how physical the job is and how skilled it is. They also know how many of the jobs exist. This means that during the Vocational Expert's testimony a lot of numbers start flying out of the Vocational Expert's mouth. If you're handling your own case, don't worry so much about the numbers, worry about the job itself and why you can't do that specific job.

---

[44] http://www.occupationalinfo.org/

MEDICAL EXPERTS

Medical experts are rarer in hearings. This is also not a good or bad sign. Some judges have them in every hearing. Other judges call in a medical expert when the judge thinks the claimant might meet a listing or the judge just needs some help with the medical records. Some medical records are far more technical than others and the judge just needs some outside expert help. The medical experts are often retired doctors who appear over the phone and usually are out of state. They will never have examined you.

Because the medical expert may find you meet a listing, the judges tend to call the medical experts at the beginning of the hearing. If the medical expert finds you disabled, the hearing is over. If this happens, thank your Judge nicely and leave. Do not question it.

If the medical expert does not find that you are disabled, the hearing will continue and the Judge will then take your testimony. Remember, the doctor is likely only an expert in one area and may not be able to comment on all areas of your disability. Keep going and tell the Judge your story.

TESTIFYING

I cannot tell you exactly what to say to win your case. But I can tell you what to do in order to guarantee that you lose your case. And that is to lie to the Judge. I cannot stress this enough. *Do not lie to the Judge.* No, seriously, *do not lie to the Judge.*

The Judge may ask some uncomfortable questions like, "It says here that you were supposed to do physical therapy every day?" or "This doctor says you would do better if you lost some weight?" Look, no one is perfect.

Just tell the truth. It's hard to lose weight when you can't move very well. Physical therapy is hard.

Often the information is more tricky. If you have a history of drug and alcohol abuse or a criminal history, this may be something that you don't want to disclose to the Judge at your hearing. Here's the problem. The Judge already knows what you don't want to tell him. He knows your criminal history and your drug history. That stuff follows you and leaves a record. It's really not that hard to find and they run a criminal record search automatically to see if you have any felony warrants and other things turn up. The Judge is asking because he wants to hear how you explain it. You know what's easier than trying to keep that out of your file - telling the truth.

So yes, at some point during the hearing you might be tempted to lie or at least fudge the truth. Please don't. It's really not worth your time. If it's something minor like not keeping up with your physical therapy as well as you should have just say so. Judges are human. They expect you to be as well. Yes, you should be doing what you can to get better, but within reason. If you throw all doctors' orders out the window, that's a problem and you're going to have to be upfront about it.

Drugs and alcohol are another story. I will tell you this. If you lie about using drugs and alcohol, you will lose. If you tell the truth about abusing drugs and alcohol but give a lot of excuses about why you did so, you'll probably lose, but you will also get a very long lecture and possibly get yelled at for several minutes. It's not fun for anyone.

Your best shot is this, "Sir, (or Ma'am,) I last used alcohol on March 25, 2012." (or whatever the actual last date was). Then shut up. Do not give an excuse. If you have a sobriety date, that is best. Own up to it. The Judge will probably ask if you are going to AA meetings or something similar. Tell the truth if you are. If you are not, you'd better not say you are because Judges like proof of these things. You still might not win, but it's your best shot of not completely ruining your case due to a drug or alcohol problem.

Judges also are (rightly) curious about where you got the money for drugs and alcohol while you were waiting for Social Security. They also really like to ask this question about cigarettes. Be prepared with an answer. Can you guess what my advice is? Right! Tell the truth!

I'm not saying that if you have a big problem in your case like never following doctors' orders or a raging meth addiction it will all go away by telling the truth. What I am saying is that if you don't tell the truth, you will blow any chance you had to begin with to get Social Security. It's one thing for a judge to approve someone who once had a meth problem in the past but is upfront and honest and is clean now. It's another to approve someone who had a meth addiction and is still lying about it. See my point?

You might also be confronted by inconsistencies in your medical record that you had no idea were there. It happens where a doctor or nurse taking down your information just gets something wrong, but now it looks like you lied about when you left high school, when you started having symptoms or worse when you last took some sort of drug. Unfortunately, there's not a lot you can do about this. If you get the file early and read it, you could ask your doctor to fix it, but honestly, the judges can pull out really minor inconsistencies that you can really easily miss. The fun part is that you had no idea the mistake was in there and you don't have an explanation for it. It's really awkward. All you can do is say that it must be a mistake. Just be aware that it happens.

For the rest of the hearing, just tell your story. Answer
the Judge's questions. Remember, the Judge hears stories
like yours all day every day so trying to manipulate the
Judge or play on his sympathies doesn't go very well.
Sob stories are not the best way to go. I promise you, the
Judge has heard stories far more pathetic and horrific
than yours. I'm sure you hate being manipulated and the
Judge feels the same way.

What the Judge wants is someone he legitimately
believes has tried really hard to get better, wants to work
and just can't. If you think about it, if you were the
Judge, that's what you would want.

Other things to keep in mind is that every judge is
different, so tips from your friends or family who have
gone through the process may not work because it was a
completely different judge. Some judges come in and go
down a list of preset questions. Other judges come in and
just talk about random things while trying to get a feel for

how you are as a person. I've had judges try to get us in and out in under fifteen minutes, others take two hours. Just remember, they all want the same thing. They want to give the money to deserving people. The problem is each judge has a slightly different idea of what deserving means.

Your economic status might also make a difference. I've had judges who prefer to award claimants who really need the money. Other judges really care about a strong work history with really good jobs. They figure people wouldn't have left those jobs unless they were really sick. Be prepared to answer questions about your finances and your past work.

Once the Judge is done talking to you, the attorney (assuming you have one) will ask you questions and cover anything the Judge didn't cover. Sometimes the Judge has the attorney do all of the questioning. Either way by the end of the hearing the Judge and the attorney both should have had their chance to ask all of the questions they want to ask. The Judge then goes to the Vocational Expert if there is one.

What you really care about is what jobs they come up with for you. Don't get angry. Everyone gets angry. Remember, the Judge isn't necessarily saying you can do those jobs. They're looking at whether you can do those jobs given a certain set of limitations. The Judge usually gives more than one set of limitations. Just ask about whether you can do those jobs if you have to be absent a lot. Or if you can't remember directions. Or if you'd need to lie down during the day.

During every hearing I have my client poking me telling me they can't do the jobs the Vocational Expert comes up with. I know you don't think you can do those jobs. That's why you applied for disability benefits. The Judge is likely going to come up with several hypothetical questions so let the Judge finish, then calmly ask your questions. Getting upset about the jobs is not going to help. Pointing out reasonably why those jobs aren't something you can do is a better tactic.

If your doctor submitted a statement about your limitations, ask the Vocational Expert if there are any jobs available with those limitations. Hopefully, there are no jobs available. Ask if there would be any work available given your testimony at the hearing.

At the end of the hearing, the Judge may or may not tell you the decision. It really just depends on the judge. Remember, you cannot tell anything by how the Judge is acting. I have lots of judges who are extremely friendly during the hearing and deny most people. I also have lots of judges who are very gruff during the hearing and point out every flaw in the case but approve most people. The only thing you can do is wait for your decision in the mail.

It is appropriate to ask the Judge how long it will take to get a decision. Usually it takes one to two months to get a decision, but it varies wildly depending on the judge and the hearing office[45]. If you have an attorney, the attorney should have a good idea of how long it's going to take. The attorney will also have online access to your case. Because the decision takes time to get mailed out, your attorney will have access to the decision about a week earlier than you will get it in the mail.

HEARING DECISIONS

Judges need to justify their decision in case of an appeal so the decision is about twenty pages. It will discuss your medical records and testimony. On the very front of the decision it will either say "Fully Favorable", "Partially Favorable" or "Unfavorable". If the decision is "Fully Favorable", congratulations! You won! Skip ahead to

---

[45] It also can vary on how Social Security is handling things as a whole and on their budget for the year. Often the length of time it takes to get a decision is out of the Judge's hands.

the chapter on what happens when you are awarded benefits.

If the decision is "Unfavorable", then I'm sorry, you did not win your case. If you want to appeal, you're going to have to go to the Appeals Council. Please read the next chapter to see what to do. Try not to spend too much time dwelling on the decision. In order to deny you, the Judge had to find you and your doctors not credible. Some judges are much harsher than others. They're going to have to pick apart your testimony and your medical records to find inconsistencies. It's just how the system works. I know that it's really not fun to read how the Judge who seemed very friendly in court is now essentially calling you a liar. I'll go into greater detail in the next chapter. You're going to take the decision personally. I understand why and I don't blame you, but a good appeal isn't about explaining why you're not a liar. Fundamentally, if a judge is going to deny you, the judge can't believe what you're saying. If you were denied, chances are the medical record just wasn't strong enough to support what you were telling the judge. The Judge wasn't necessarily saying that you made everything up, just that your records don't show that you are as disabled as you say you are. My best advice is read the decision then talk to your attorney about what the best course of action is. Don't read the decision over and over. It won't do you any good.

If the decision says "Partially Favorable", then one of two things happened. One option is the Judge thinks you are currently disabled, but not from the date you said you were disabled. The Judge moved your date of disability to a later date. Sometimes the Judge discusses this with you in the hearing. This is called an amended onset date. The reasoning for this is usually because there was a change in your medical condition. You might have tried working and failed. Sometimes the decision seems pretty random. The good news is that you're approved and you will be getting continuing benefits. There will be less back pay and your Medicare benefits start later[46]. You're approved and you don't need to fight Social Security anymore unless you want to[47].

The other option is that the Judge thinks you were disabled when you went out of work, but that you can work now. This is called a closed period. You get your back pay but you don't get continuing benefits and you don't get insurance. I usually see this when someone had a big surgery, was fighting cancer, had a stroke, or some other major medical condition that then improved. Again, the judges usually discuss this during a hearing. The plus side is that you may be ready to go to work and

---

[46] Remember, your Medicare benefits start two years and the sixth month after your date of disability. If the date moves, so does your Medicare start date.

[47] You can appeal an amended onset date but you run the risk of losing the benefits you just got approved.

you'll have several months' worth of benefits to put in the bank.

You have three options with a closed period. First, you can say, "Actually, yes I am ready to go back to work! I will take that money and enter the workforce once again!" Second, you can appeal the decision. Again, this will be covered in the next chapter. You risk the Appeals Council deciding you were never disabled to begin with and having to pay back the benefits[48]. I would discuss this with an attorney to see how great the risk is. Third, you can refile for benefits and start over again. Your benefits that you just won will be safe and you can go for future benefits.

---

[48] See Chapter Nine on Overpayments.

CHAPTER SIX: "HOW MANY APPEALS CAN THERE BE?" THE APPEALS COUNCIL AND FEDERAL COURT

If you've gotten denied at a hearing, you're now in the realm of the Appeals Council. You're no longer proving current disability; you're proving that the Judge did something wrong. It's not a good argument to just say, "The Judge didn't believe me or my doctors and thought I was lying and I wasn't lying!" This is why if you didn't get a lawyer before, you really need to talk to one now. Your arguments need to be based in specific laws and not just "I'm sick and I can't work."

APPEALS COUNCIL

To file with the Appeals Council, you need to file a form HA-520. It can be found at http://www.socialsecurity.gov/forms/ha-520.pdf. Like

before, you have sixty days to file your appeal. The form

needs to be completed and sent to:

Social Security
Office of Hearings and Appeals
5107 Leesburg Pike
Falls Church, VA 22041

I would send the request certified so you have proof that

you sent it. This is not an appeal that you can submit

online, and it is possible the paper appeal could be lost

and you want proof that it was submitted.

The actual Request for Review is one page. Technically

you can file this one page request and the Appeals

Council can look at your case and decide on their own if

the Judge did anything wrong. Realistically, you want to

give them some guidance. If you have an attorney, the

attorney will write a brief to the Appeals Council

detailing what it is the Judge did wrong and citing the

record with the appropriate laws. This is going to be

difficult for a non-attorney to do. If you really still want to do this on your own, you can submit a letter to the Appeals Council explaining what it is you think the Judge did wrong.

The Appeals Council only has one office in Falls Church, Virginia and acts as a clearing house for the entire country. They have multiple branches in that office, but they are still very, very busy. Expect it to take at least a year and probably more to get a decision back. The wheels of justice move slowly. If you have an attorney, the attorney will have online access to your case and can tell when the Appeals Council receives your case and will be able to get the decision about a week before you receive it in the mail. If you choose not to have an attorney, you're going to need to call about a month after you send in your appeal to make sure they have it. Unlike the hearing level, you will not receive anything telling you the Appeals Council received your appeal. Until you get your decision, you will receive nothing from the Appeals Council. Their phone number is 877-670-2722.

While you are waiting for a decision, you are not supposed to submit new evidence. This is the hardest thing for my clients to accept. The Appeals Council does not care about your current medical condition. They are looking to see if the Judge made a mistake. Therefore, they are looking at what the Judge had available at the hearing. The Judge did not have your current medical records to look at. Do not bombard the Appeals Council with your current records.

You also can't submit a new application while you're waiting at the Appeals Council. Only in very rare circumstances is this allowed[49]. You're stuck waiting. This is occasionally why some people choose to submit a new application rather than filing an appeal because they

---

[49] Ask your attorney.

think they will be approved faster. The problem is that you're never guaranteed an approval with Social Security and you lose the back pay from your prior application. This is why you really want to consult an attorney at this level to see what is best for you.

The decision from the Appeals Council will be fairly simple. They have three options. First, they can approve your case outright. This happens very rarely. I would not rely on this for your case. It occurs in a tiny percentage of cases but it does happen.

Second, the Appeals Council can also remand the case back to the Judge. This means that they found the Judge made an error and they are sending the case back to the Judge to fix the mistake. Read the decision carefully. Your case will be sent back to the hearing office. You will probably have the same judge for your remand hearing. Sometimes the judge has moved or the judge isn't available or you have moved and you will end up with a different judge.

The second hearing is often much different than the first hearing. You'll want to update all of the medical records before the hearing. The Appeals Council may not care about your current medical treatment, but the second hearing will cover what has happened since the first hearing. Because the Judge has already taken your testimony the first time, much of the usual parts of the hearing can be skipped.

The Appeals Council often orders the Judge to use a Medical Expert or a Vocational Expert if one was not used the first time. They will also order more testimony taken about a specific medical condition or previous job. The Judge will probably focus the testimony on very specific things. Your attorney will also update the Judge on your new medical conditions. If you have a different

Judge, you will likely do all of the testimony over again so the Judge can assess your credibility.

Again, it's good to have an attorney for these cases to make sure that everything is done properly according to the Appeals Council's Order. The hearing might be much shorter than your first hearing. In my experience, the judges are usually not happy that the case got sent back from the Appeals Council, but they behave professionally and try to make sure the case is handled properly according to the Order. I wouldn't spend too much time worrying that the Judge is going to take revenge on your case and deny you just because the case got remanded.

Once again, remember that you're there for disability and credibility still matters so tell the truth and be respectful. Do not be smug that you won at the Appeals Council. The Judge still has to approve you and he has the final say. Everything else works the same as the other hearing. You still have to wait for the decision.

The third option the Appeals Council has is to deny your Request for Review. When they make this decision, they do not explain why. You just get your denial and are left with the question of what to do next.

FEDERAL COURT

Not all Social Security attorneys handle Federal Court appeals. It's not the sign of a good or bad attorney. Some just choose to focus on the lower levels of Social Security. You have sixty days to file an appeal.

Federal court appeals are more of an undertaking for your attorney, so it's best to know what it entails. First, attorneys' fees go up. If they didn't go up at the Appeals Council, they definitely go up for Federal Court. Most attorneys will still work on contingency but they will take a larger amount of your back pay, generally 25%.

There is also the matter of Federal Court filing fees which at the moment are $400.00 per case. Your attorney is probably not going to front that money for your case. You will need to come up with $400.00 or file what's called an In Forma Pauperis which is a form you fill out about your finances explaining to the Court why you can't pay $400.00.

Then there's the fact that Federal Court cases are extremely time consuming for your attorney. Your attorney will need to file a thirty page Opening Brief with the court and then another fifteen page Reply Brief. Every attorney is very picky about the cases taken to Federal Court. Do not be offended if your attorney does not want to take your case to Federal Court. Your attorney may believe wholeheartedly that you are disabled, but there may not be strong enough legal issues in the decision from your hearing to justify the hours spent on a Federal Court case.

If you've been stubborn enough to go this far without an attorney, I really cannot recommend that you take on a Federal Court appeal without an attorney. The Courts try to be fair to Appellants without an attorney, but it is really a miserable process that is near impossible to win alone. Attorneys charge a contingent fee. Go and talk to one. It costs you literally nothing to go and consult one since Social Security attorneys do free consultations. The chances of you hiring me are extremely slim geographically speaking, so I'm not trying to drum up business for myself. I am telling you honestly that handling Federal Court alone without knowing what to do and what arguments to make is just not a good idea for anyone.

From filing to decision, Federal Court usually takes about six months to a year with the average being about eight months. It really depends on where you are. Much like the Appeals Council, the Court has the option of approving you, denying you or remanding the case.

If the Federal District Court denies you, you can appeal to the Federal Court of Appeals, then to the Supreme Court. Again, this is the job for an attorney.

If you choose not to file in Federal Court, you can refile a new application. Actually, you can refile a new application while in Federal Court. You need to be careful, because you have to prove that your condition has substantially worsened since your hearing. It may also have changed substantially if you have reached an important birthday like 50, 55 or 60.

Remember there's always another appeal, but each successive appeal becomes more complicated. Be sure each step in the process is the right step for you. Find a lawyer you can trust and who explains the process and your options in a way you are comfortable with. Don't get discouraged. The road is long. But that doesn't mean you won't get there in the end.

Chapter Seven: "I got awarded! Now what?" How payments work

You got awarded! Congratulations! Let's have a talk about what happens next.

When Disability Determination Services determines someone should receive benefits at the Initial Application or Reconsideration levels, the case gets sent to the local office for processing part of the case and the payment center for processing the check. If there is no additional information that Social Security needs to process your case, you might find out you won by checking your bank account and discovering a large chunk of money has been deposited with no notice. The actual award letter comes about a week later.

If Social Security does need more information, it's usually a copy of your birth certificate, your bank information for direct deposit, or to confirm your finances if you have an SSI claim. *If you get a call from Social Security asking for this information, call them back immediately[50]!!!!!* You do *not* want to wait on this call and have your case put at the back of the line.

Some people do not have a bank account or do not have money to open a bank account until they get their money from Social Security. Instead of issuing checks, Social Security now issues Direct Express debit cards. Every month, they will load your Social Security payments onto the card. You can continue to receive your payments this way if you so choose. Social Security tries to stay away from the paper checks they used to send out. They now require a bank account or the use of the Direct Express card. _____

[50] You should always return their phone calls, but this call should not wait until tomorrow.

BACK PAY

The best part about getting Social Security benefits aside from getting money every month is the large chunk of back pay. If you only applied for and received SSDI (which remember is based on your past work and not need-based) you will get all of your back pay at once.

If you receive SSI, which is need-based, you are only allowed to have $2000.00 (or $3000.00 if you are married) at one time. But your back pay is likely much more than that. Social Security handles this by giving it to you $2000.00 at a time, letting you spend it down and giving you more every six months until the amount is gone.

This sounds fairly wasteful to me. You're just supposed to blow all this money? How is that good for anyone? You're allowed to ask for it all up front if you have a good reason for it like paying off debt. And let's face it, anyone waiting for Social Security and qualifies for SSI probably has debt.

You can also put the money into a special needs trust. Remember when we discussed those in Chapter One? The special needs trust can take your back pay and put it into a trust so you can use it for things you need like a car, dental visits, clothes, emergencies or whatever you need. You have to pay to have the trust set up, but then you're not blowing the money on nothing. Remember my tip though - please have an attorney who specializes in these trusts handle the trust, not just an estates and trusts attorney. A trust that is set up incorrectly by your friend who knows about wills is much more expensive than just doing it properly the first time.

SSI ACCOUNTING

The less pleasant part of SSI is that once a year you have to account for how you used the money. Remember, SSI can only be used for food and shelter. Once a year you have to fill out a form about how you used the money. The form isn't that complicated so it's nothing to worry about, but you do have to do it. If you forget to do the accounting, you run the risk that Social Security may stop your payments.

You also have to inform your local office within ten days of the next month when you earn any money or have a change in your living arrangements. If you do not, you will have an overpayment or underpayment issue and those are miserable to deal with. This isn't just about you either. If you are married, your spouse also has to report wages to Social Security.

AWARD LETTERS

Once you are awarded, you will receive an award letter from Social Security. In fact, you may receive several. The award letter will tell you how much back pay you are getting, how much they reserved for your attorney's fees, and how much your monthly amount will be. It will also tell you when your monthly check will be deposited. Monthly checks are deposited on the first, second, third or fourth Wednesday of each month. This is determined based off of what day of the month you were born on.

If you had an attorney, the attorney will be paid directly by Social Security. Sometimes the attorney is paid before you sometimes the attorney is paid after you. There is no pattern. But you should not be responsible for paying your attorney out of your check. If your attorney is asking you to write them a check, read your award letter carefully to make sure Social Security did not withhold attorney's fees. In my experience, attorneys are really good about not double billing from Social Security and their client, but everyone makes mistakes so just double check your award letter. Your attorney's fees should only come out of the back pay and not your continuing benefits. If you are confused about what your fee agreement covered, ask for a copy from your attorney.

If you are receiving both SSDI and SSI you will receive two award letters. Often if you applied for disability right after you stopped working, you will receive SSI for the first five months of your disability before SSDI kicks in. Once SSDI starts and you're making more than $730, you do not need to do the accounting for SSI any longer.

If you are receiving SSI and your income changes or your spouse's income changes, you will receive a new award letter every single time explaining your new benefit amount. This means that in some cases you could get a new award letter every single month.

TAXES

After you've been awarded, the next logical question is, "Wait! I just got a bunch of money! Do I need to pay taxes on this?" Well, kind of. The government is actually pretty nice here. They do not want you to give back all of your hard-won money in taxes. The taxes do get a little complex, however.

For the first year after you won, you really should have a Certified Public Accountant do your taxes. The reason for this is that your back pay is probably going to cover more than the past year. Your taxes are going to have to be amended for the past couple of years so the back pay can be included. If your back pay was included just for the year that you received it, you would be thrown into a higher tax bracket and you don't want to do that. You count the back pay for the year that you technically earned it, which means you have to amend your prior years' tax returns. This makes filing taxes more complex than normal. This is also why you should probably ask your friendly local accountant to help with your taxes. You just don't want to deal with it. It's less expensive and much less work to file properly the first time. Also, you just spent lots of quality time fighting with Social Security. Do you really want to fight with the IRS? No. You don't.

As for the year where you earned your income, a lot is going to depend on if you have other income. If your only income is Social Security, then you're fine. This is because if your household income is up to $25,000 including *half* (and only half – don't worry about the other half) of your Social Security benefit, you don't have to pay taxes on your Social Security income. If all you have is Social Security income, you're certainly not receiving $50,000.00 from the government so you don't have to pay taxes on it.

If you have some other income or you have some investments that are paying money, you may be over the $25,000 mark. If you are married, then you have up to $32,000 (including half your benefit amount) and you still don't have to pay taxes on your benefits.

If you are single and you make between $25,000 and $34,000, you have to pay taxes on 50% of your benefits. If you are over the $34,000 then you pay taxes on 85% of your benefits. The income that is not from Social Security is taxed normally.

If you are married and you make between $32,000 and $44,000, then you pay taxes on 50% of your benefits. If you are over $44,000, then you pay taxes on 85% of your benefits. Again, any non-Social Security money is taxed normally.

Look, I get that taxes are really confusing when it comes to Social Security. Even if you're in a year when you didn't receive back pay, it's probably a good idea to use a program like TurboTax if you're doing your own taxes to make sure the calculation is correct. When in doubt, talk to an accountant. That's what they're there for. Once you've done your taxes for a year or two they won't seem quite so confusing, but please get help the first time.

REPRESENTATIVE PAYEES

Sometimes Social Security or the judge in your case is worried about your ability to handle the payments on your own. In those cases Social Security asks for a representative payee. This is someone who receives the checks on your behalf and pays your bills with the money. The payee can give you some of the money to spend, but the payee needs to have control of the money.

A payee is always ordered in cases where the disabled person is a minor. One is also ordered if the disabled has some sort of psychological issue where Social Security is concerned about an ability to use the funds properly. For example, they order one if the person has a low IQ, has shown an inability to take care of oneself, can't count change, can't go shopping alone, doesn't know how to pay bills, etc. A payee is also ordered if the disabled person has shown to have bad judgment either due to the disability or past decisions. Some people with bipolar disorder go on spending sprees when they are manic. If the disabled person has a criminal history the Judge is uncomfortable with, a payee may also be ordered.

This isn't necessarily a bad thing. Social Security and the judges really just want to make sure that if they're giving money to a disabled person that the money will be used properly. They don't want to hand over cash to someone who doesn't know how to use it to pay for rent and groceries and can't remember to pay bills.

Who do you pick to be a representative payee? This is not a decision made by Social Security. The disabled person must decide themselves. Usually it's someone close to you like a family member. Remember this person will be intimately involved in your financial affairs. You need someone you trust and who you feel comfortable calling when you need money. It also needs to be someone you trust not to take your money and use it for themselves. If you don't have someone that you trust, or simply don't want to put anyone in your life in that position, there are companies that act as representative payees as well.

Once you have someone that you want to be your representative payee, you need to have that person fill out form SSA-11. It can be found at http://www.socialsecurity.gov/forms/ssa-11-bk.pdf. The payee will need to open a bank account specifically for the Social Security checks. Once a year, the payee will also need to account for how the money was spent.

If you think Social Security made the decision in error and you really don't need a representative payee, you can ask for Social Security to make the payments directly to you. You must fill out the same form, SSA-11 but request to be made your own payee and explain why. It will help if you have a note from your doctor explaining why you are competent to handle your own money. You can also request to become your own payee at a later date if you think your condition has improved enough to handle your own money. Just be aware that if you are telling Social Security that your condition has improved they will probably want to assess whether or not you are still disabled.

CHILD'S BENEFITS

Good news if you have children under 18 and you're receiving SSDI[51]! You get more money! Social Security recognizes that children cost money and they can bump up your benefits by up to $600.00 a month. An individual child gets about $200.00 a month, depending on how much the disabled person gets. Children's benefits are paid when you have children in your custody. This is not the same as the disabled children's benefits discussed in Chapter One. Your children do not need to be disabled to get these benefits. To get the children's

[51] Unfortunately there are no children's benefits for people receiving SSI.

benefits, you need to go to your local office with their birth certificates and complete the children's benefits form with them.

What if you're divorced and do not have custody of your children? It gets a little sticky. If you do not have custody of your children and are not paying child support, your child's parent who has custody can receive the child's benefit. This way you are providing some child support in your own way. If you are providing at least one half support, you can get child's benefits.

Fun fact – if you have overdue child support and there is a judgment against you, your SSDI can be seized to pay that outstanding child support. Just so you know.

Adopted children are treated the same as natural born children, of course. If you have legal guardianship of a child, you can receive child's benefits. If you are a grandparent who is taking care of a child and is considered the guardian, you can receive child's benefits. Step-children also get children's benefits if the parents have been married more than a year. If your child is still in high school, you can get child's benefits up to the age of nineteen.

Also be aware that if you have a child, but they are not currently with you because they are in foster care or have been taken out of the home by Child Protective Services, you cannot receive child's benefits during that time because the government is already paying for them to live.

If you're not sure, the rule is generally that if the child is legally your responsibility and you're paying the child's expenses, you can get Child's Benefits for the child. Just ask Social Security when you fill out the Child's Benefit Form.

Payment Problems

Unfortunately, sometimes things don't go according to plan. Social Security has lots of moving parts and payments don't always come through like they should. If you have an attorney, the attorney should handle your payment problems. Hopefully your attorney has much more experience dealing with these issues than you do. But, sometimes you have to deal with these issues on your own and you might have problems getting payments in the future.

When you get paid by Social Security, the payments are processed through Payment Centers. The local office is not the place that authorizes your SSDI payments although they do authorize your SSI payments. Once you're on monthly payments they tend to be issued smoothly[52]. Problems come getting the payments to begin. Back pay is where most of the problems start.

---

[52] The exception is if you change your bank account. This is going to

If you get your award letter and you don't have your back pay, first give them a week or two. Different branches and offices move at different rates. Don't go sitting on hold forever if there's no reason to. But while you wait, do some troubleshooting:

- Did you give Social Security your bank information?

- Did you give Social Security the *correct* bank information?

- Have you checked your bank account? (You'd be surprised how often this one comes up)

- Have you changed banks or accounts since you first filed?

- Did you bring into Social Security a copy of your birth certificate?

- Have you checked your mail for a Direct Express debit card?

- Did you move recently?

- Do you have a problem with mail getting stolen?

---

be a headache. Don't close your original account until the deposits are made into the new account. Even then I might give it another six months or so before closing the account.

If you've now waited two weeks after your award letter and you still don't have your back pay, it's time to start digging. The first place you need to call is your local office.

If you're getting SSI only, the local office is going to authorize the payments. If it's SSDI as well, the payment center authorizes the payments because it comes out of a different fund. Again, do NOT call the national 1-800 number! The local office will be far more helpful. Just call and tell them that you were awarded and you don't have your back pay yet. They should be able to tell you what they're waiting on. It may be something simple. The local office will likely send a message to the payment center. They will then tell you that you will be paid, "Within three months." This is code for, "We're working on it. Please don't call us daily."

If you still don't get paid within about a week and a half, call again. This time ask for a manager. Keep calling. It should be sorted out quickly. If you really can't get paid and they won't explain to you why, you can always contact your congressperson.

INSURANCE

One of the benefits of getting approved for Social Security is that it automatically comes with insurance. If you are approved for SSDI, you are approved for Medicare two years and the sixth month after your date of disability. Please note this is *not* the date that they approve you for disability. It is the date they found you unable to work and is usually the date you stopped working. Double check your award letter or the decision from your Judge. Social Security often takes about two years to get so in theory you should be getting close to getting Medicare around the time you are approved.

Medicare will start automatically. You will get cards in the mail before it starts along with a packet on how it works and what parts you want to sign up for. Medicare is good insurance but sometimes people have insurance through their spouses or other means so you can opt out if you want to. Social Security will deduct the premiums for Medicare from your check. For Medicare parts A and B in 2016 the cost is $104.90 a month[53]. If you are already past the two years and sixth month period when you are approved, you can pay past Medicare premiums and submit medical bills to Medicare to be paid. You can also look into Medigap insurance which will pay any medical expenses that Medicare doesn't cover.

If you are eligible for COBRA from your previous employer and you get SSDI benefits before it runs out, COBRA will extend from its usual eighteen months to when Medicare starts for you. Be sure to notify your insurer as soon as you have the favorable decision from

---

[53]http://www.medicare.gov/your-medicare-costs/costs-at-a-glance/costs-at-glance.html

the Social Security so your insurance coverage doesn't terminate.

But what about before you qualify for Medicare? The good news is that with Obamacare, you cannot be denied for insurance. It still might be expensive depending on your situation. If you have no income you can get extremely low cost insurance through https://healthcare.gov. You can also check through regular insurance brokers to see what sort of deal you can get.

Once you're approved for SSI or SSDI before Medicare starts, you qualify for your state's medical insurance. Because you're not qualifying for it the usual way, you cannot be cut off due to the whims of the state legislature. The insurance is likely not as good as Medicare, but it's better than nothing. You will need to contact the office yourself and tell them you were approved for disability benefits.

Different states offer other benefits for people who are approved for Social Security benefits. It doesn't hurt to see what else is available if you're still struggling financially. If you don't understand something about your benefits call your local Social Security office.

Chapter Eight: "What if I want to work?" Working while receiving benefits

No one wants to think that they are going to be on disability forever. Luckily, Social Security doesn't want to pay you forever either so they make it as easy as possible to try working while getting disability benefits. Before you try working, you need to know how the system works.

First and foremost, you are on disability for a reason. Don't try working because you're bored if you can't handle it. Ask your doctor if you can try working and what is recommended. Should you try full or part time? What are your restrictions? Try doing a similar amount of activity at home before you even apply for jobs. There is no sense hurting yourself or making your condition worse. Make sure that it's something that you can reasonably do on a regular basis. A failed work attempt is nothing to be ashamed of but it's just good sense to try to make sure you can handle it before you apply. I also have clients who try volunteering for a bit before they go back to work to see how they handle it. You have options.

Substantial Gainful Activity

You're allowed to work a certain amount without it affecting your disability at all. It's called Substantial Gainful Activity and we've talked about before in regards to whether or not you were working according to Social Security's definition. That holds true now as well. You're allowed to earn $1130[54] without a problem. Just remember that if you're receiving SSI you have to report the money and they will deduct $1.00 for every $2.00 you

---

[54] As of 2016.

make over $20.00. *But*, they will still consider you disabled as long as you don't make a penny more than $1130. By Social Security standards you might as well not be working at all.

Here's where you need to be careful and where I keep seeing people slip up – do not get paid every two weeks. Twice a year you will go over the $1070.00 amount and that *is* considered work. What happens then?

TRIAL WORK PERIOD

You're allowed to try working without losing your disability. What if you tried going back to your old job and two months in you discover that you just can't do it? But now you've lost all of your disability benefits and ruined everything! No one would try working. And as we discussed before, Social Security would really like you to go back to work.

Therefore, we have the trial work period. You're allowed to earn over $1130 for nine months in a five year period before your disability stops. The months do *not* have to be consecutive.

This is why I'm warning you about getting paid every two weeks. Because after four and a half years you're going to hit that ninth month of earning over $1130 and your benefits are going to stop suddenly. You will be baffled about why your work is suddenly a problem. Except now you won't because I'm telling you that it's a problem.

Social Security assumes that nine months are enough for you to figure out if you're well enough to work and for the work to be sustainable. You may have some false starts in there but by the ninth month you should be able to keep going. The good news is you'll be able to draw a paycheck from Social Security and your new employer for nine months while you see if you can work.

Insurance

Your Medicare coverage keeps going for 93 months (that's almost 8 years!) once you return to work[55]. You can keep paying your premiums and Medicare will keep you on their books. It's really in Social Security's best interest if you're well enough to work and part of that is making sure you can see a doctor. In case you haven't guessed, Social Security *really* doesn't want you to have any reasons not to try returning to work.

If your new employer has insurance, you can keep Medicare as a secondary insurer just in case. I would recommend doing so if you're concerned you won't be able to keep working. It's never a bad idea to have more insurance than you need versus less. You can't get back on Medicare if you're back at work and give up Medicare.

---

[55] http://www.socialsecurity.gov/disabilityresearch/wi/detailedinfo.htm#TWP

SSI and Medicaid (aka your state's insurance, remember?) are a little more complicated. You need to

- Have been eligible for an SSI cash payment for at least 1 month;

- Still meet the disability requirement; and

- Still meet all other non-disability SSI requirements; and

- Need Medicaid benefits to continue to work; and

- Have gross earnings that are insufficient to replace SSI, Medicaid and publicly funded attendant care services.

This gets complicated. Basically you're working enough to not be on SSI anymore, but you're not earning enough make up for the amount of SSI plus insurance. To make it a bit easier, there's a chart Social Security puts out. You can find it at

http://www.socialsecurity.gov/disabilityresearch/wi/1619 b.htm. If you're making over the amount, you lose your Medicaid.

What if you can't do what you used to do, but you think with a little training that you could do *something*? Again, Social Security would love for everyone to go back to work so they have their own vocational rehabilitation agency called Ticket to Work.

As it happens I am a huge fan of vocational rehabilitation. Ideally, they run you through a battery of tests from psychological to manual dexterity. They're really looking to see both what you'd be good at and what you'd like to do. Their goal isn't to put you in a job that you would hate because you're not going to stick in that job for very long. From what I've seen, vocational rehabilitation often puts people in much better jobs than they had before with very little training.

If the vocational rehabilitation counselors work with you and if they find that you can't do any work, then it bolsters your disability claim and any continuing disability reviews in the future. It happens. You are on disability for a reason. However, you're far better off working in a job you enjoy then staying home and being disabled.

Social Security may refer your case over to the Ticket to Work program. I've had judges refer cases after they approve them for disability. Once you're approved, you can also request to be evaluated by the Ticket to Work program.

The Ticket to Work program also works with employers to place the workers with companies who get tax incentives for hiring disabled workers. More information can be found at http://ssa.gov/work. Or you can call 1-855-835-0010.

Subsidies and Impairment Related Work Expenses

Sometimes employers make special concessions so they can hire the disabled. We all want to encourage employers to do this. I've seen this a lot with family-run businesses who want to have a family member around and make sure the disabled family member has some extra money to live on. The disabled family member may be paid the same as the other staff members, but do far less work.

The problem comes in when it starts messing up the disabled person's disability checks because they're making too much. Luckily, Social Security helps us out here. Social Security looks at the special conditions to determine if the work is actually substantial gainful activity. They do an evaluation to see the actual market value of the services and then determine if it's equal to substantial gainful activity. The amount above this is called a subsidy. It still may screw up the SSI portion of disability. But for the substantial gainful activity analysis, Social Security will look at the actual market value of the services and generally the disabled person will be allowed to stay on disability. The employer will need to discuss the disabled person's actual job duties with Social Security, but it's a nice program to encourage disabled people to work.

The other thing to pay attention to is any expenses paid so you can work. Let's say you need an expensive back brace or physical therapy twice a week in order to work. Social Security will deduct the cost of that from your wages. The deduction may bring you under the amount for substantial gainful activity.

It's only fair. If you have to incur expensive medical costs solely so you can work, you shouldn't have to bankrupt yourself and end up worse off than before. This is why it's very important to keep records of your medical costs. These costs should be covered by insurance but if you have out of pocket costs that you have to cover in order to be functional enough to work, Social Security will deduct those costs from your income to see if you are over the $1130 amount for substantial gainful activity.

FAILED WORK ATTEMPT

That's all fine and good, but what if the attempt at work doesn't go so well? You were on disability for a reason after all. Or what if your health fails again? Or the stress of working makes you sick again?

These are all normal concerns. Social Security doesn't want you to worry about these things when you try going back to work. After all if you tried going back to work and immediately lost your disability benefits and had to go through the whole process again, who would ever go back to work?

If you stop working because of your condition within five years you will get expedited reinstatement of your disability benefits. You just need to reapply, remind Social Security that you were on benefits before and you stopped working because of the same condition. Then you will be placed on your benefits again. You will need to show that you stopped because of your same medical condition and not some other reason and your case will move quickly to reinstatement.

This means that while you're working, you should still be seeing doctors and keeping copies of your medical records. It's always a good idea anyway, of course. Aside from trying to stay as healthy as possible, you want a complete record of your medical history in case you go out of work again. Even when you are back at work, you still want a good relationship with your doctor regarding your limitations and your overall condition. You might need accommodations from your employer and you'll need documentation for that. You also don't want to overdo it and be right back at home again. Plus the work attempt makes you far more credible in Social Security's eyes because they know you want to work.

The important thing to remember is that Social Security really, really wants you to work so they make it as easy as possible to go back to work with little or no consequences to your disability payments. If you think you can work give it a shot and see how it goes.

Chapter Nine: "Social Security wants how much back?" Overpayments"

I won't lie to you. Overpayments are miserable and most attorneys won't take overpayment cases. The best method of dealing with overpayments is to avoid them all together. How do we avoid overpayments? By understanding how they come about in the first place.

An overpayment happens when you either should have stopped receiving Social Security payments or you should have been receiving less money but your payments continued at their normal rate. You will get a letter in the mail out of the blue telling you that you owe thousands of dollars to Social Security and that they would like a check immediately. The natural reaction is then to panic.

As a lawyer, let me tell you how I look at the problem. Do not be fooled by Social Security's language. They tell you that you can file a waiver of overpayment if you don't think it was your fault. Let's clarify what they mean by that. Everyone clings to hope on that language. You should not.

Social Security assumes that you know all of their regulations[56]. Therefore, they assume you *should* have known if you were getting overpaid. That's why it is your fault that you were overpaid even if it took Social Security a couple of years to notice it.

You can use the argument that it's not your fault if you have a representative payee. You might also be able to use that argument if you can prove you have some

---

[56] Just so you know, their regulations are online and are about 60,000 pages.

cognitive difficulties. Otherwise you're going to have

deal with the fact that it's your overpayment problem.

So, let's figure this out. Is it a legitimate overpayment?

Let's go over some reasons why you might have been

legitimately overpaid:

- Have you been working and on SSI and not told Social Security?

- Have you been working and earning over $1130 for longer than nine months?

- Are you on SSI and receiving any money over $20 and not told Social Security?

- Were you in jail, prison, or a government-run institution for more than thirty days and not told Social Security?

- You are getting retirement from Social Security and are still working and earning over $41,400.[57]

- What about any of the above situations where you told Social Security but your check amount didn't change?

_____

[57] Social Security offsets $1 for every $3 made over $41,400 if you're working after you start receiving retirement benefits.

These are pretty standard reasons for getting overpayment notices. If this is the case, you're sunk. The overpayment is likely valid. Even if you told Social Security about the payments, if your payment amount didn't change, you're still responsible for the overpayment.

Let's talk about reasons why you might not be overpaid. Social Security makes mistakes, too[58].

- Someone else is working under your Social Security number so it looks like you were working even though you're on disability benefits.

- You did not actually earn the money they say you earned (alimony, child support, stock dividends, etc.)

- Currency exchange problems (i.e. the money is coming from another country and the exchange rate is wrong)

- They have your case confused with another case.

---

[58] I know! Can you believe it?

- You accidentally reported the wrong information

- Special needs trusts problems/misunderstandings

- The money they say you earned is exempt – it counts as a subsidy or it goes towards medical treatments that allow you to work[59].

It is well worth your time to take a look at the overpayment and see if you can make your income low enough to fit under substantial gainful activity if that is the problem. Social Security isn't great about explaining why you're in overpayment status. They tend to be very angry about them. I have people call me several times a month in panic mode because they got the overpayment letter. Almost all of them are legitimate overpayments. You should *never* pay the overpayment until you understand why you were overpaid.

If you were legitimately overpaid and you now understand why, you do not have to write Social Security

---

[59] See previous chapter.

a giant check unless you really want to[60]. Instead, fill out the Request for Waiver of Overpayment. It can be found here: http://www.socialsecurity.gov/forms/ssa-632.pdf. You will put in your financial information and ask for a payment plan.

It's amazing. As soon as you agree to a payment plan, Social Security will become so much nicer about your overpayment. They will agree to a low monthly payment as long as you're paying something.

Most attorneys won't take overpayment cases as I mentioned before. The reason is that most of the cases are legitimate overpayments. I won't negotiate those for clients for the very simple reason that I just don't think Social Security will believe my client has no money for repayment if they're paying an attorney to negotiate for them. Plus Social Security is pretty easy to deal with

---

[60] Why would you want to?

once you agree that you'll do a payment plan. It's really not a great use of your money to pay an attorney to negotiate this.

Now you might be able to find an attorney to take your legitimate overpayment case but they're few and far between. If your benefits have stopped because of the overpayment issue and they should be reinstated once it's sorted out, you might be able to do a contingency agreement with the attorney. Otherwise you're stuck doing an hourly rate with the attorney which can get expensive.

If it's a legitimate overpayment, you need to file a Request for Reconsideration. The form can be found at: http://www.socialsecurity.gov/forms/ssa-561.pdf. Explain why your case is not a legitimate overpayment. Then you're going to have to come up with proof depending on the situation. These don't get sent to Disability Determination Services. Social Security handles these at the local office. It's hard to get anyone at Social Security to deal with these because, like attorneys, Social Security hates dealing with these as well. Can you blame them?

Once you finally get Social Security to make a ruling, if it's negative, you then need to ask for a hearing with a judge. Yes, this is another administrative hearing with an administrative law judge. You'll actually get some traction here although they don't like dealing with these either. The important thing is to be able to show that your information is correct and that the overpayment is not actually an overpayment.

Do *not* file both a Waiver and a Request for Reconsideration. You are stuck choosing one path or the other. Make sure you can prove your case. This is why you really need to determine if it's a real overpayment or not.

STOLEN SOCIAL SECURITY NUMBERS

If someone has stolen your Social Security number, there are a few things you need to do. First, you need to contact the police. You don't need to call 911. Call the local police department and have the police fill out a police report. Social Security will want a copy of it.

You also need to contact the Internal Revenue Service. They have a specific form for this. http://www.irs.gov/pub/irs-pdf/f14039.pdf. It's the Identity Theft Affidavit. Complete it and keep a copy. Also notify your credit cards and put a notice on your credit report.

Of course you need to tell Social Security. They will conduct their own investigation. Sometimes it's really easy to tell what's going on. You probably weren't working in Phoenix full time at the same time you were working in Austin. However, if you're out on disability and someone is working under your number, it can look like you're the one who's working. This is when it gets sticky.

Do NOT do your own investigation. This isn't your job. You can hire a private investigator if you want, but you do not want to start calling up employers or trying to find the person yourself. Social Security will go through the employment history with you and you can identify with employers you actually worked for. They will then contact the employers that you did not work for and ask for more information. Often the employers have copies of driver's licenses and other identifying information. Sometimes the job is something you are not qualified for. It can and will get sorted out but it can take a long time.

UNDERPAYMENTS

Yes, the urban legends are true. Sometimes Social Security makes a mistake in your favor. Trying to get them to admit it is another story. Usually the underpayment happens because a person is entitled to more than one benefit. It's very hard to mess up a simple SSDI case. When a person is entitled to SSDI, SSI, has children, then retires and his wife gets spousal benefits, things might get a little complicated. There are also a lot of difficulties when a person dies and figuring out who gets what benefits gets complicated. This is particularly true if some members of the family are disabled. It becomes quite a mess.

If you think there might be money left on the table, the easiest thing to do is just to go into Social Security and make sure you're getting your maximum benefit. Social Security is good about going through the numbers with you to make sure you're getting the right amount each month.

If a person was owed money at the time of their death, you can collect that as well if you are their direct heir.

The right to that money doesn't die with the claimant. Of course you cannot get continuing benefits; but the past benefits can still be paid out. You can ask for those benefits well after their death.

Fun Fact – If a person has paid into the Social Security system, their heirs can collect $255 from Social Security if they report the death to the local office and bring in a death certificate.

You might also be entitled to back pay for child benefits if your parent was getting disability benefits while you were a child and just didn't file for them. Prove you're the child of your parents by showing them your birth certificate and give proof that you were living with them at the time.

Just writing letters will not work. You are going to need to go into the local office and ask for your past due benefits.

CHAPTER TEN: "I HAVE TO PROVE I'M DISABLED AGAIN?" CONTINUING DISABILITY REVIEW

This is the envelope that strikes fear in every disabled person's heart. I get a lot of calls about Continuing Disability Reviews (CDRs) all saying, "They're going to take away my benefits!"

Well, no. Probably not. Social Security is going to see if you're still disabled. When someone is approved for disability benefits, Social Security isn't going to approve them forever. Did you really think they would? Or should? At some point, someone needs to check in with you to see how you are.

When you're approved for disability benefits, the person approving you also decides when you need a CDR. The average is every three years. It can be as low as six months or as long as seven years. If you think about it, this makes sense. You could have a surgery coming up that might make you better. There could be medication changes that might improve your condition drastically. Or you might be a quadriplegic with no hope of improvement. The quadriplegic probably doesn't need someone looking in on him every year to make sure he's still in bad shape. But the person who just had surgery probably does need someone checking in to see how it went.

Social Security isn't out to get you with these reviews. You've already gotten through the hard part. Relax and tell them what they want to know which is – are you still disabled?

The first part of the CDR is just a form they have you fill

out[61]. It's not that different from the function report you filled out when you were first applying for disability. They just want to know how you're doing. What are your days like? How is your condition doing? Are you still going to doctors? (Unless you have a permanent condition that genuinely doesn't require going to doctors like mental retardation, please go to doctors.)

Like before, if you're young, they may be gunning for you more than if you are nearing retirement age. It's just a fact of life and economics. It also depends on your condition. Mental illnesses are more likely to change and get better than degenerative illnesses. Some of it is also just going to depend on who gets your case for review.

Just be honest and tell them what's been going on. Since now you've been disabled for awhile, your condition has probably deteriorated or even more likely, it's stabilized.

---

[61] Social Security loves forms if you haven't noticed.

You've learned to live with it and you know your limits. You probably have fewer bad days because you know what's going to bring them on. In some cases you may be more active because you know exactly how much activity you can handle. With luck, you might be less depressed because you've adjusted to your situation. It's okay. We expect this. Just be realistic about your abilities in your CDR paperwork.

In most cases, this will be it. You won't hear anything until the next CDR comes around so you can go ahead and relax.

If Social Security feels like they need more information, they will send you again to a consultative exam with one of their doctors. Yes, you get to go to another one of Disability Determination Service's doctors once again! I know it's what you've been waiting for. You still don't need to panic. Chances are you just haven't seen a lot of doctors and they're just checking up on you. It might also be that something wasn't quite clear and they wanted more information.

It works the same way as before. You'll go to the appointment. You'll explain any changes that have occurred. If the doctor doesn't know what your medical condition is, you'll explain it. Remember, Social Security already found you disabled, so you don't need to worry here. Just tell the truth.

A few weeks after the appointment, you'll either find out that you are approved for continuing benefits or that they are stopping your benefits. If you're approved for continuing benefits - congratulations! If Social Security is stopping your benefits, continue on to the next section and keep breathing.

Request for Reconsideration of Cessation of Benefits

When you get the letter that Social Security is stopping your benefits, you need to act quickly[62]. The letter will say that you have sixty days to appeal and that is correct. But you have *ten* days to request the appeal and have your benefits continue during your appeal. By this point in the process, you may have noticed that it takes several days after the date on the letter to actually get anything in the mail from Social Security. The letter also isn't very clear that you need to file your appeal within ten days to keep your benefits coming in while you appeal which is why I'm stressing it now.

If you get the notice that your benefits are stopping, go *immediately* to your local Social Security office to file your appeal. You can't do it online and I wouldn't trust

---

[62] Without panicking please.

the mail to get it there in time. You need the appeal to get there within ten days and you need proof that it got there.

The benefits for your kids will also continue if you get the forms in to Social Security on time. Your insurance will also continue.

Now it's possible you might not want the benefits to continue while you appeal. Who in the world would choose that? There are some decent reasons to choose that. If you don't win your appeal and Social Security chooses to cut your benefits, you're going to have to pay back the benefits to when they first cut you off. Then you're stuck with an overpayment case, which, as I've mentioned before, are miserable.

You might also want an attorney's help. If you don't continue your benefits while you appeal, then there's back pay accruing that you can pay your attorney with. If you're getting your benefits then the attorney has to be paid an hourly rate. You may or may not be able to afford that. Most attorneys are going to want a retainer (an advance on their fees) before they will help you with these cases. So there are some legitimate reasons why people might choose not to have their benefits continue while appealing their cases. You have to figure out what is right for you.

If you're not worried about continuing benefits then you don't have to rush down to the local office and you can mail off your appeal within sixty days and just double check that Social Security got it. You can elect to have just your Medicare continue while you appeal.

The form you file to appeal your case is a Request for Reconsideration, but it's not the same form as before. The form is found at http://www.socialsecurity.gov/forms/ssa-789.pdf. Please check that you want to appear at a hearing. You'll also

need to fill out a Disability Report found at
http://www.socialsecurity.gov/forms/ssa-3441.pdf.
Again, you'll need to fill out the medical releases for
Social Security. You can find them here:
http://www.socialsecurity.gov/forms/ssa-827.pdf.

Next, your case will get sent to Disability Determination
Services. It's a little like when you first applied for
disability benefits. An examiner will look at your case
and gather the medical evidence.

This time they will call you in for a disability cessation
interview. The examiners aren't doctors or judges so
they're less formal than when you went to court before.
They want to know about your life and disability.
Honestly, it's the same questions you normally answer –
what can you do and what can't you do? You may or
may not want an attorney for this part. Most attorneys
take these cases unless there's an issue with fees as

discussed above. If you want to try it on your own, you can do that, too.

You should have an answer a few weeks after your interview with the examiner. The examiner might decide to send you for another consultative exam. It's a little harder to give a time frame for how long these disability cessation cases take because they vary wildly depending on the case. Sometimes the examiner gets the case, realizes that the person should absolutely be on disability and approves it within a day or two of being at Disability Determination Services. Sometimes it's there for several months. It just depends on the examiner.

DISABILITY CESSATION HEARINGS

If you're denied at the Reconsideration level, go ahead and file for a hearing. Use the paper form at http://www.socialsecurity.gov/forms/ha-501.pdf and fill out the same disability report and 827s. You will then need to plead your case to an Administrative Law Judge. It works the same as other disability hearings so you can read the chapter on those. This is really a time when you would want to consult with an attorney if you haven't yet.

You have to wait in the normal waiting line for a hearing. There is no jumping the line just because you're a disability cessation case. Try to remember that they found you disabled once and think positive. I would spend extra time looking at the file if you are trying to handle it alone to see why they feel you are not disabled now. Generally as people get older it becomes easier to get disability so there should be something in the file that shows why they think you are no longer disabled.

If the judge thinks you are not disabled anymore, you can always appeal it to the Appeals Council, but you are not going to continue to receive your benefits. If you were still receiving benefits, you now have an overpayment case. Start talking to your local office about a payment plan and look into your insurance options.

SURVEILLANCE AND FRAUD

I get asked from time to time, "Is Social Security going to come to my house and watch me?" Probably not.

They certainly do have a fraud department and they are very vigilant about anyone they consider to be taking advantage of the system. Perhaps you've noticed my opinion about telling the truth? Social Security really tries on the front end not to approve anyone who isn't truly disabled. People do get through sometimes and Social Security has to deal with them. In no way are there large numbers of people on Social Security who are faking their disability like the news will have you believe. There just aren't. I've done this job a long time and I talk to a lot of other attorneys around the country[63]. These

---

[63] I'm chatty, okay?

giant groups of people faking disability just aren't getting through anywhere.

Social Security wouldn't be doing their job if they didn't have a fraud department and there is a department devoted to finding people they think are defrauding the system. The fraud department is called the Office of the Inspector General.

Let me be clear. If you are getting a Continuing Disability Review or you are getting your benefits cut off, that doesn't mean they think you're a fraud. It means they think you're getting better and not disabled anymore. If they file criminal charges against you for fraud, you can be sure they think you're defrauding the system. Are we clear on this?

There are a number of ways you can come to the attention of the Office of the Inspector General. Social Security can see something in your file that seems like a problem. It could be that it mentions you have a past criminal history of defrauding government entities, or you show signs of faking your injuries, or you're drug seeking, or your symptoms don't make sense, or your symptoms are wildly different every time you see a doctor. It's not like Social Security has a ton of money for surveillance and investigation so they have to really have some decent proof before they go looking in to your case. It's easier just to deny you or cut you off.

Another option is that they have had a complaint about a person[64]. If Social Security gets a complaint that a person is on disability but is digging ditches, playing football and doing lots of things a person with a back injury shouldn't be doing, they might send the Office of Inspector General out for surveillance. This really isn't a regular occurrence so you should not spend your life

---

[64]Please don't use this as an excuse to complain about your neighbor who you don't think should be on disability. You don't know their situation and you don't want someone doing that to you.

paranoid that Social Security is watching your every move. Again, this is why I tell people to tell the truth. If you're telling the truth, then it doesn't matter if Social Security is watching you. It's a little creepy, but it's not going to result in any loss of benefits.

Another area the Office of the Inspector General handles is problems with checks. Specifically, when they go to the wrong people. If representative payees are not distributing the checks properly or keeping the checks for themselves that's a fraud issue. If a person dies and no one tells Social Security and the family keeps cashing the checks, that's fraud.

The Office of the Inspector General handles counterfeit checks and Social Security numbers. This can be tied to immigration problems and even terrorist groups. They handle bribing Social Security employees, pretending to be Social Security employees[65], and crimes involving SSA employees. The Office of the Inspector General handles them all.

If you think you've come across fraud and want to report it, the Office of the Inspector General's fraud hotline is 1-800-269-0271. Please do not use this number unless you're really sure that a fraud has been committed.

Fundamentally, once you're on Social Security disability, people tend to stay on unless they get better and go back to work. Keep up with your medical treatment and make sure it's documented. Never ever ignore mail from Social Security and you'll be fine.

---

[65] Please don't try these.

Chapter Eleven: "What if my case isn't perfect?" Drugs, Alcohol and Crime

You started reading this chapter just because you wanted to read about drugs and crime, didn't you? I'll admit it's more fun than overpayments.

If you don't buy into the idea that Social Security Disability has a bunch of fakers on its payroll, then of course you believe it's a bunch of drug addicts, right? It's not really. If you're currently using drugs it's very difficult to get disability benefits. I'm not going to say it's never happened, but it's going to be really, really hard. Now what I will say is that if you have a drug and alcohol history, we may be able to deal with that.

Are you surprised? Let me start by saying that I am not now, nor have I ever been, nor will I ever be a supporter of drug use or crime. Your case will be far, far, far easier to win if you have no drug or alcohol usage or criminal history in your past. If you are thinking of applying for disability benefits and you are using any drugs that are not prescribed for you, or overly using the drugs that are prescribed for you – stop now. I'm fully aware that these are an addiction and if it was that easy to stop we wouldn't have any addicts. Presumably you're reading this for the best chance at winning your case. So, if you want the best chance at winning your case, stop using illegal drugs. Also stop drinking alcohol and smoking. Stop using marijuana if it is legal in your area.

I can tell you what Social Security's standard for drugs and alcohol is. Basically it is if you stopped the drugs and alcohol, would you still be disabled? Another way of putting it is: are they in any way material to your disability? You're thinking then, "Why do I need to

stop?" Practically speaking, Social Security and the

judges really want to see what you're like without the

drugs and alcohol which means that you need to quit for a

substantial period of time. This is why I'm telling you to

quit now.

I realize at first glance it seems strange that Social

Security is even willing to have past drug users or

alcoholics[66] on their disability payroll. A straight no

drugs ever/no criminal history/no alcohol abuse policy is

going to leave an awful lot of really sick people out of

luck.

A ridiculously high percentage[67] of schizophrenics,

bipolar, and psychotic patients have a history of drug use.

---

[66] Not all alcohol drinkers are alcoholics – we're not concerned with the people who only have a drink here or there. Relax.

[67] Over one half according to the National Alliance on Mental Illness. http://www.nami.org/Content/NavigationMenu/Inform_Yourself/About_ Mental_Illness/By_Illness/Dual_Diagnosis_Substance_Abuse_and_M ental_Illness.htm

It's very simple – before they were diagnosed they knew something was wrong and they try to self-medicate. Not to mention that serious abuse in childhood often leads to serious mental illness and doing drugs and alcohol is often a coping mechanism. Once people are properly medicated, the drug and alcohol use often stops. I'm not saying it's a great choice to use drugs and alcohol regardless of the situation. I'm saying it happens and we don't refuse disability benefits to very sick people because they have it in their past.

There's also the fact that people apply for benefits at all ages and sometimes people have a past. Poor decisions in the past shouldn't have to ruin someone's chances at disability benefits.

However, it really is best to make it clear that your drug and alcohol use is in the *past*. Not to mention that alcohol is a bad mix with almost every prescription drug. I can't even imagine what a terrible combination street drugs and prescription medications are. Seriously, don't even think of doing that. You won't need disability because you'll be dead.

The other thing to remember is that drug and/or alcohol use comes up all the time in medical records. Far more than you might realize. When you start seeing a new doctor, you complete forms and they usually ask how much you drink alcohol. Your doctors also usually ask you regularly. That makes it into your record. Your doctor may also ask you about illegal drug use both in the past and currently. Social Security examiners and judges pay a lot of attention to these parts of the record and make a lot of notes if the answers aren't the same across doctors. They will ask about any inconsistencies in your hearing.

You could lie to all of your doctors to try to keep any drug usage out of your record, but that's a really bad idea for a few reasons. First, that's an awful lot of work to keep straight. Is this really your game plan? Drug and alcohol use comes up all the time. Second, this is extremely dangerous. Doctors aren't asking for fun and curiosity. Drug and alcohol use is linked to all sorts of illnesses. Your doctor will have a much harder time diagnosing and treating you if you don't give an accurate medical history. Isn't the point of going to a doctor to get better? Third, there are lots of medications the doctor won't give you if you're taking certain drugs or drink a lot. Even if your drug history is way in the past, you're still better off telling the doctor. Just tell the truth.

Lying about current drug use is also spectacularly stupid because doctors are trained to be able to diagnose addicts. You're going to have a hard time getting the doctor to believe you about anything if you're lying about using drugs or alcohol. This means it's going into your record that you appeared to be on drugs and lied about it. Your doctor is probably going to test your urine or blood for drugs anyway. Not to mention judges and even your attorney can probably tell if you're on drugs as well. I know I can usually tell even over the phone. Now you've ruined your case because you've been labeled a liar in your medical records so you're not getting disability anyway. Lying about your current drug and alcohol use is not a great plan.

What should you do aside from not taking drugs or drinking alcohol? Tell the truth. We really need a period of sobriety as long as we can get but for a minimum of six months. Go to Alcoholics Anonymous or Narcotics Anonymous meetings if you can. To find a meeting, go to http://www.aa.org/ or http://www.na.org/. If you can't go to a meeting, try to spend some time on the internet in online addiction forums. Make sure you have a sobriety date. Judges love sobriety dates, but it's also a fantastic way for you to measure your progress[68]. If you're a

---

[68] Alcoholics Anonymous is a classic for a reason. If you think you have a problem, why not check out a meeting? They're free and

veteran, the VA system has a lot of good programs for drug and alcohol recovery. Try to do something to show you're serious about recovery if you're recently sober. Quitting cold turkey does not usually impress judges if it's recent.

I'm of a mixed mind on urine drug screens. It's nice to have them to show sobriety, but if you're choosing when and where to do them it just doesn't show much about your sobriety. Even if the attorney chooses when to have the client do the urine drug screen, I wouldn't be very impressed. There are so many drugs that don't stay long in your system[69] and alcohol isn't usually caught unless you've just stopped drinking. I just don't think they help much. A blood test or hair test is more helpful since they capture a longer period of time, but the judge doesn't know who actually did the testing and under what

they're everywhere.

[69] I'm not telling you which ones! What kind of book do you think this is?

conditions. If your attorney tells you to go and do a drug test absolutely do it. Just don't assume that you can prove your sobriety by getting a urine drug screen before your hearing.

ALCOHOL

Alcohol is a little weird because it's legal. You're allowed to drink alcohol, don't get me wrong. A glass of wine here and there is not going to ruin your claim for disability benefits. A six pack of beer every night might. A bottle of vodka will cause problems. Some of this is also going to depend on the judge. Most judges drink alcohol and that likely skews their opinion. It's like the old joke, "The definition of an alcoholic is anyone who drinks more than I do.[70]" If you have a heavier drinking judge, you're probably not going to get dinged for a few beers here and there. But a judge who hates drinking and

---

[70] Do NOT quote that during your hearing.

doesn't think anyone else should drink is going to be harder on you.

It's also really going to depend why you're disabled. If you're disabled due to alcohol usage, you really need to stop drinking to get disability. Actually, you really need to stop drinking anyway as I'm sure you're aware. The rule says you can be disabled because of the behavior but as long as you are still disabled if you stopped, then you can still get disability. For example, if you have cirrhosis of the liver from drinking or alcohol-related dementia, you can get disability. Practically speaking, the judges are going to be a lot happier about giving you disability if you have stopped drinking.

This isn't something you should get paranoid about. The judges just want to know that you are doing everything you can to get better. That includes not drinking heavily. If you tell your doctor how much you're drinking and your doctor thinks you should cut back, you should.

Everyone has an opinion on how much alcohol is too much. Again, almost every medication isn't supposed to be mixed with alcohol. It's never a bad idea to stop drinking while you're applying for disability.

TOBACCO

If you want to annoy a judge, this is one of the best ways to do it. It's not quite as good as lying in court or being rude to the judge but I rarely see a subject that so many judges get angry about as smoking. They really, really hate smoking. I don't mean smoking in court, although that is a terrible idea. Judges just despise smoking in general.

It's particularly bad if you have lung or heart problems. Just accept you're going to get a long lecture about smoking if that's your disability. Judges also tend to ask a lot of questions about how claimants afford cigarettes when they have no money for food or housing. It's a valid question and you might want to think about how you'll answer.

Aside from lung problems, smoking is bad for just about every part of you. Judges really take this subject personally. I know it's legal and it's your body. But if you want to win your case it might be time to try quitting again.

MARIJUANA

Because of marijuana's quasi-legal status, this one gets a little tricky. See, even in states where it's legal, it's still not legal on the federal level. Social Security is a federal program and the judges are federal judges. Marijuana as of 2016 is still classified as a schedule 1 controlled substance which is the same status as cocaine and heroin.

If you had some great dream of coming into court and lighting up a joint in front of a federal judge...well that's not going to go well[71]. For one thing, courthouses are smoke-free workplaces. Technically you can still be arrested and charged under the federal statute for possession of marijuana. Just so you know. Don't make a judge mad on this issue.

Now it's pretty unlikely that the judge will have someone there to arrest you at your hearing because you smoke marijuana. The judge can't give you a free pass because it's legal in your state. At best, a judge has to treat it the same way he treats alcohol and tobacco. This means that just because it's legal doesn't mean that you should be smoking huge amounts of pot any more than you should be drinking a bottle of vodka a night and thinking it won't affect your disability benefits.

There's also the question that comes up just like it does for cigarettes which is - how are you paying for the marijuana? Judges really don't like the thought of paying

---

[71] Also get some better dreams.

benefits to a person who's just sitting around getting high all day and spending government money on pot. If you really want your benefits, try not to use marijuana recreationally while you're applying for benefits.

But what about medical marijuana you ask? That's an excellent question. In my experience there are two types of medical marijuana users. The first is the person who medical marijuana was designed for: the truly sick person who never used marijuana in his life but has huge amounts of pain or nausea and whose regular physician prescribed or recommended the marijuana. That person is reading this section and getting very nervous. Relax. I won't say there's no judge in the nation that won't still give you problems for using medical marijuana[72] but you're likely fine.

---

[72] It's probably a good idea to consult a local attorney on this to see if the local judges are exceptionally hard on the marijuana issue.

The other type of person using medical marijuana is the person who went immediately to the dispensary the second it opened and got a prescription from the doctor there and has a long history of using marijuana recreationally. It's not that you don't have legitimate medical issues, but you would be using marijuana regardless of your medical issues. The judge can see right through you. It's quite a big sign that your medical marijuana is being prescribed by a different doctor than all your other medications and has not been recommended by your regular doctor. I'm not saying marijuana can't be helpful for certain medical conditions. I'm saying getting a medical marijuana card is not a get out of jail free card for people who want to use it recreationally. Marijuana might have a fairly legal status but you don't need to be using it recreationally. Marijuana users continually argue that it's not addictive so why don't you prove that by not using it recreationally while your case is pending.

PRESCRIPTION DRUGS

This is another tricky one. Almost everyone applying for disability has some sort of chronic pain and they're going to need pain killers. But painkiller abuse is huge. Where do we draw the line? The judges and Social Security do not want to approve a bunch of drug addicts. Unfortunately the fact remains that if you're on narcotic painkillers for a long time, you're going to be dependent on them.

Let's be very clear. Dependent is not the same thing as addicted. Dependent means you will have physical symptoms of withdrawal when you stop taking the pills. It's the same thing for coffee drinkers when you stop drinking coffee and you get a headache. An addiction is an emotional withdrawal and you have destructive behaviors associated with it. You can have an addiction without a physical dependency. You don't need to go to rehab because you're trying to drink less coffee.

Your doctor will prescribe pain killers and when you stop taking them your body will notice. That's normal. If you start going to other doctors and exaggerate your pain so you can get more painkillers after your doctor refuses to give you more – then you have a problem. Do you see the difference?

Social Security is really careful about claimants with drug seeking behavior. They want to know if you're faking or exaggerating your symptoms to get more painkillers. Not all painkillers are addictive or will make you high. There are a lot of painkillers you can ask for that won't have any issue with addiction. This is really important for recovering addicts.

What you don't want is to be labeled a drug-seeker. Your case is going to be ruined in that case. It's going to be really difficult to come back from that. Unfortunately it can happen accidentally. Let's say you throw out your back and the only thing that worked last time was the

muscle relaxant Flexeril and the pain killer Oxycodone.
This time you throw your back out on the weekend and
you can't call your doctor's office. So you go down to
the local Emergency Room. If you tell them, "I threw my
back out, can I have some Flexeril and Oxycodone?"
Congratulations, you're a drug seeker! It's now in your
file and you'd better not go back to that hospital or any
office or hospital associated with that hospital ever again
because you'll be treated like a drug addict.

I'm not trying to make light of drug addiction. It's a
serious problem and you need to be careful when you're
prescribed addicting pain killers. Really think about
whether you need to take that pill when you reach for that
bottle so it doesn't become automatic. If you think you
might have a tendency towards addiction, talk to your
doctor about non-addicting painkillers. But you also
need to be aware of how easy it can be to be labeled a
drug-seeker without knowing it.

People around you may also be addicted to painkillers who you may not suspect. If you repeatedly get your medication stolen, it also is very suspicious to your doctors and Social Security. Invest in a medication safe if you need to. They're your pills and your doctor prescribed them for a reason. Be careful.

If you think you may be developing an addiction, talk to your doctor immediately. You're far better off saying, "Hey doctor, I think I like these pills too much, can we switch me to something else?" than staying quiet about it. If it gets too far, the bravest thing you can do for yourself and your loved ones is to seek help. Forget your disability case, people die all the time from prescription drug overdoses. It's not something to take lightly. Getting help will not ruin your case.

When it comes to illegal drugs, you need to be really honest with your doctors. Social Security doesn't have much patience for street drugs so you need to show a consistent period of sobriety and a firm sobriety date. Judges pay very close attention to your timeline of drug usage. Because there are so many diseases associated with narcotics, you need to be really clear with your doctors about what exactly you used and when. Your doctor needs to know if you shared needles, smoked drugs, or took pills so he knows what to test you for.

It's important to remember that you're not the first and you're not the last person your doctor, your lawyer and the judge have seen who has done all these things. They've seen it all. All they want is the truth. It takes effort to surprise doctors, lawyers or judges. They only really get annoyed when you lie.

The judge is deciding if you are disabled *now*, and part of that is seeing if you are honest about your past. If you can't be honest about past drug use (which the judge likely already knows) then the judge isn't going to believe anything else you say. Just tell the truth.

Don't forget, if you did enough drugs, there's likely another record of it...in your criminal file.

CRIMINAL HISTORY

When you apply for benefits, Social Security asks if you have any open felony warrants for your arrest. I've never been able to understand why anyone would apply for government benefits when hiding from law enforcement. You cannot get benefits until your warrants are cleared. Aside from just felony warrants, the judges are well aware of your criminal history by the time you have a hearing. Your criminal history is generally discussed during your psychological consultative exam as well. As an attorney, I run my potential clients' names through the court database looking for criminal activity before I take them on. It's all on the internet and we know where to look. It's just not that difficult to find a criminal history.

As we discussed before, people make mistakes and it's not the end of the world to have a criminal history. A lot of times people with mental illness also often have a criminal history when they are not properly medicated or have undergone a lot of abuse. It happens. The best thing to do is to be honest about it. Tell your attorney and be really clear about what you did and why you were incarcerated. No one feels any better about your incarceration when you try to avoid telling people why you were in prison. Tell the truth, please. We don't need details of the crime. Just tell us what you were convicted for.

Just so you know, if you are incarcerated or in jail over thirty days while you are receiving benefits, you will not get paid by Social Security until you are released. It's because the government is already paying for you to live so you do not get Social Security at the same time. The benefits should start up again when you are released. If they do not, contact your local Social Security office.

If you are incarcerated while applying for benefits, you need to notify Social Security and your attorney immediately. Sometimes they will even have a hearing for you while you are in jail. The jail will either transport you to the hearing or let you testify over the phone. Again, you won't get paid during the time you are incarcerated but you can receive back pay and the payments will start when you are released.

TESTIMONY

It's never going to be fun to testify about your substance use or criminal behavior. I bet you've read enough of this book to guess my opinion on the matter. Can you guess? That's right! Tell the truth! But I'm going to give you a bit more than that. Do *not* give excuses for your behavior. The judge doesn't want to hear how you only smoked meth because you were having a really bad day that day. It implies that the next bad day you have, you might just smoke meth again! Or you stole that car because the owner did something bad to you. What happens when someone does something bad to you again?

Say, "I last smoked methamphetamines on _____" and give a date. Then *shut up*. This is why I like a sobriety date. Take responsibility for your behavior. It's the same thing for criminal behavior. You made a mistake, now live with it. Giving justifications for your behavior is going to result in a long lecture and perhaps some yelling. No one wants that[73].

---

[73] Including your attorney.

By the way, this is actually decent advice for when anyone asks you about drugs or alcohol. No one wants to hear your bad justifications for why you did drugs. Everyone is happier when you take responsibility for your actions. Just a bit of life advice from me.

IMMIGRATION PROBLEMS

Here's how this can come up. You can be in the country legally working on a green card and pay in to the Social Security system. Then your green card can expire or you can have other immigration issues and no longer be in the country legally. You might be entitled to Social Security benefits, but have an illegal status. It's not quite fair. If that's the case, I wouldn't recommend applying for benefits. In general, if you're hiding from the government, applying for benefits isn't a great idea. Depending on where you are, Social Security may or may not refer you to Immigration, but do you really want to take that chance?

There's always the chance that you may or may not know that you are not here legally. You might not know your green card has expired. If your green card has expired, you may still have some options.

Depending on where you're from, our government has a reciprocity agreement with other countries where your earnings here count towards their Social Security programs and vice versa. You can find the list of countries here: http://www.ssa.gov/international/agreements_overview.html. You can also cure your green card deficiency and then you're fine. Contact an immigration attorney if this is the case.

If you're a refugee, you might be able to apply for SSI. Certain classes of refugee or victims of human trafficking are allowed to apply. This gets really complicated and a bit beyond what I want to handle here. If you think this may apply to you, go ahead and call your local office.

Fun Fact - if you are an immigrant and want your family to qualify for benefits quickly, you can join the United States Armed Forces. Your immediate family may then qualify for SSI benefits without having to work the five years required for SSDI benefits.

SOCIAL MEDIA

Your case is going to depend a lot on how you present yourself. Most conditions are diagnosed by your self-report. Quite frankly, in order to get good treatment and disability benefits your doctor and judge are going to have to believe you. You therefore need to think about what you're putting out there into the world.

I won't say all, or even most judges will Google you to check your tweets or Facebook. But it definitely happens. You have to realize that when someone checks your online accounts, there isn't always an easy way of knowing that the rock climbing photo you just posted was taken three years ago. We all have a tendency to post only the good things about our life online.

If your doctor or the judge doesn't think you're being truthful about your activities it only takes a minute or two to check up on you online. You need to be really careful about what you post. Make all of your accounts private to the public. Make sure there's nothing online that you would mind a judge seeing. I don't suggest you complain constantly on Facebook about your pain every day. That's certainly not necessary. Just be aware that it may be more than your friends reading your posts.

Chapter Twelve: "Aren't there other benefits I can get?" Long Term Disability, Veterans' Benefits, Workers' Compensation

Let's talk about how some other benefits affect Social Security. It's not often that Social Security exists in a vacuum. There are some other benefits that often come up with Social Security and it's helpful to know how they work.

Long term disability benefits

Let's get one thing straight – if your employer offers you long term disability – *take it!* It's a fantastic benefit and it's generally really cheap when offered by an employer. It can be about ten dollars a month or less. It's a lot more expensive if you have to buy a private policy. Each policy is different so I'll have to speak in general terms.

There are long and short term disability benefits. Whereas with Social Security you have to expect to be off work at least a year, there's no such limitation for short term disability benefits. It's specifically there for when you have surgery, have a baby, or have a prolonged illness. It's usually three to six months long and ends either when you go back to work or when long term disability kicks in. Usually you just need a note from your doctor saying you can't work.

Long term disability usually kicks in at either three months or six months. Once again, you need a note from your doctor saying you shouldn't be working. Unlike Social Security, they're just looking at whether you can do your current job or a job that would pay the same amount. They also pay about 66% of your salary (depending on the policy) but you don't pay taxes on it.

Depending on the company and the case manager, long term disability can be a really easy ride or a really difficult one. It's also going to depend on why you're disabled. You also want to get a copy of your insurance policy. Some are only for two years, others change the disability standard to whether you can do any job after two years, and some stay with the same disability standard until retirement. Others change the time period depending on the disability, so if you're out for a mental illness it's only two years. You will want to know what to expect.

The one thing they almost all have in common is that they want you to apply for Social Security benefits. They usually have a clause in their policy that says they can make you apply for benefits and when you're approved, they can offset your benefits by the amount you're receiving from Social Security. This means that instead of getting your full benefit from the insurance company, you'll get your Social Security check and then the insurance company only has to pay you a little on top of that to equal your original amount from your policy. Unfortunately, this also means they will ask for any back pay you receive from Social Security as well. They won't ask for your attorney's fees[74] but the rest goes to the insurance companies.

Nevertheless, those insurance checks are close to your salary amount and will keep you going while you wait for Social Security to come through. It is definitely a benefit you want. Their standard of disability is much easier to meet than Social Security and they take the word of your doctor. If this is a benefit your employer offers, take it!

VETERANS' BENEFITS

Both veterans' benefits and Social Security benefits are federal programs. This works out very well for disabled

---

[74] Most insurance companies have their own Social Security attorneys they work with.

veterans. If you have a disability rating from the Veterans Administration (VA), due to some court cases, in most of the country Social Security has to pay attention to the disability rating. The technical term is they have to give it "great weight"[75]. So if the VA has rated you fully disabled, which is 70% and over, Social Security has to pay attention to that, or find a very good reason not to.

Social Security is also working on the Wounded Warrior project. If you have a 100% disability rating and you were wounded in active military service after October 1, 2001, they'll expedite your disability case. For more information see http://www.ssa.gov/people/veterans.

---

[75] See McCartey v. Massanari, 298 F.3d 1072 (9th Cir. 2002); Chambliss v. Massanari, 269 F.3d 520, 522 (5th Cir. 2001); Brady v. Heckler, 724 F.2d 914, 921 (11th Cir. 1984); and De Loatche v. Heckler, 715 F.2d 148, 150 n.1 (4th Cir. 1983).) And one circuit court said that VA disability ratings were entitled to "substantial weight." (Kane v. Heckler, 776 F.2d 1130, 1135 (3d Cir. 1985).

Workers' Compensation

Unfortunately, because workers' compensation is a state-run program, Social Security doesn't have to pay attention to any rulings they make. Even worse, they offset for workers' compensation payments. You cannot receive more than 80% of the monthly earnings you received while you were working from workers' compensation and Social Security combined per month. Your monthly earnings should have already been established by the workers' compensation court.

This gets really complicated because your workers' compensation may change while you're waiting for Social Security benefits. It gets even worse if you are offered a lump sum benefit from workers' compensation. You have to be really careful about lump sum benefits because if you're not Social Security will treat it all as wages and offset your Social Security benefits accordingly. This may not be fair because that lump sum may be partly attorneys' fees or earmarked for medical treatment or past due doctors' bills. You really don't want money that you didn't receive being taken out of your Social Security check. Therefore, if you get a lump sum from workers' compensation make sure the insurer designates how they came to that amount and what each portion is for. If you have a workers' compensation attorney, they know to do this and can give you a breakdown.

UNEMPLOYMENT

Unemployment is a mess when it comes to Social Security. I understand that you might have been laid off from your job and that you need to pay bills. I won't even tell you not to apply for unemployment. But here's the problem: to get unemployment, you have to say that you are ready, capable and willing to work. To get Social Security, you have to say that you can't perform any job. Do you see the issue?

In the past few years Social Security has really cracked down on this and now they're trying to be consistent and say that you cannot receive disability benefits for the same period you get unemployment benefits. This is not to say that you can't apply for Social Security benefits while you're getting unemployment benefits. Social Security will just change your disability onset date to after you stopped receiving unemployment benefits.

It causes problems with judges who may find you less credible since you told two different stories to two different government agencies. You might also have a problem finding an attorney since there will be less back pay and therefore less attorney's fees.

You have to live somehow while you're waiting for Social Security to come through and most attorneys understand this. I will never be the one to tell you not to file for unemployment. I will however let you make an educated choice about what it means for your Social Security case.

STATE DISABILITY BENEFITS

Some states also offer disability benefits similar to Social Security. Unfortunately, you can't just run off to those states the second you become disabled[76]. You have to have paid into the state's disability system and worked in that state before you became disabled[77]. The states that offer their own disability program are:

- California - http://www.edd.ca.gov/disability/disability_insurance.htm

- Hawaii - http://labor.hawaii.gov/dcd/home/about-tdi/

- New Jersey - http://lwd.dol.state.nj.us/labor/tdi/worker/state/sp_clt_menu.html _____

---

[76] That would be great though, wouldn't it?

[77] Check with the individual state for how long you need to have worked and how recently.

- New York -
  https://www.health.ny.gov/community/disability/

- Rhode Island - http://www.dlt.ri.gov/tdi/

- Puerto Rico -
  http://www.trabajo.pr.gov/pdf/sinot/SI-1SolicitudBeneficio_SINOT_ING.pdf

These programs can be hugely helpful while you are waiting for Social Security to process your case. Their standard of disability is generally easier because they pay you less and for a shorter period of time.

Be aware that Social Security offsets for these state disability payments. It works the same way as workers' compensation where your combined income from state disability and Social Security cannot exceed 80% of your pre-disability income. The reason is that Social Security doesn't want you to earn more on government benefits than you were making while working.

Remember to keep good records of the money you receive from any benefit because Social Security (and the

IRS) is going to want to see how much you made when the time comes to pay you.

CHAPTER THIRTEEN: "HOW DO I SURVIVE?" RESOURCES

Because it can take two years or longer to get disability benefits the question I get most is, "How do people survive?" I respond back "Any way they have to." It's also why I try to give people a realistic time frame for how long it will take to get benefits so people can plan.

Some states are much better places to be disabled in than others. You're always going to be better off being near friends and family who can help you out. If you're not living near your loved ones now, you might want to think about moving. Emotional support can be worth a fortune.

INSURANCE

Fortunately, Obamacare means that no one has to be without insurance. Go to the website https://www.healthcare.gov or call 1-800-318-2596 for help signing up for insurance. It might not even be necessary to go through Obamacare if you have more funds available. After Obamacare was enacted, no insurance company can refuse you for preexisting conditions - but they may be expensive. You can also get quotes from insurance agents on what might be the best insurance for you. I wouldn't try to figure it out on my own. That's what insurance agents are for.

Get your insurance and stay on it. If you lost your insurance and it's not during open enrollment – that is a qualifying event and you can still sign up for insurance right away. Keep going to the doctor and follow your doctor's advice.

PRESCRIPTIONS

If you have trouble paying for your medicine please tell your doctor! They often have closets full of samples they can give you. Your doctor can also prescribe a generic alternative or a similar but less expensive drug. You can try http://www.needymeds.org/index.htm. It's a website that lists all the medications and the pharmaceutical company associated with them. Most drug companies offer programs to give discounted or free medications to disabled or needy people. Be sure to check around to different pharmacies because some offer better deals on prescriptions than others.

WELFARE/CASH ASSISTANCE

The rules for welfare change from state to state. For some states you can only get on cash assistance if you have children living at home with you. You may qualify for help with utility bills and water. Cash assistance is

run through your state's Department of Economic
Security. You will need to call your utility company
yourself and ask for help with your bills. In addition,
there is state and federal housing for the poor and
disabled. Some of this is also run through their state
mental health programs so if you are seeing a counselor,
the counselor might know how to put you in touch with
those programs. Most importantly, if you can get in
touch with a social worker, it will greatly help you
because every area has different programs.

A call to the bank that holds your mortgage may also
result in some help. Often mortgage companies have
policies or programs to help people and you might be
able to miss a few mortgage payments without a problem.

An internet search is the best way to find organizations
that help disabled people. There are also specific
organizations that help people with specific diseases.
Food banks, Goodwill, St. Vincent de Paul, United Way

and local churches are a great way to find people to help even if it's just finding someone who might drive you to doctor's appointments or help clean your house.

Don't forget that if you are in California, New York, Hawaii, New Jersey, Rhode Island or Puerto Rico, you can file for state disability benefits while you're waiting for Social Security to kick in.

The government runs a website called https://www.disability.gov/ that contains a lot of information with help for disabled people. Below is state by state information that can help you get started with finding resources. By no means is it an exhaustive list.

The government runs a website called https://www.disability.gov/ that contains a lot of information with help for disabled people. I have an entire section on my website, http://fosterlawaz.com that I continually update with resources for people waiting for disability because this information changes all the time. Google is an excellent resource because you can find what you need and the information is at your fingertips. I also tweet resources regularly at @fosterlawaz.

On my website, I also include state specific resources for people. I use what I call catch-all sites. You can find all sorts of information on these sites for whatever you need if you don't know where to start. Food stamps, housing, insurance, and whatever else you might need if you are just screaming to yourself, "I need help now!".

Honestly, the ultimate answer to "How do people survive?" is to do the best you can. Everyone's situation is different, but you're not the only one waiting for benefits who has no money. This makes Social Security fairly unsympathetic to your situation. Or, if not unsympathetic, just know that you're not special. They can't treat your case as special just because you're running low on money. Social Security has to expedite only the most extreme cases.

The important thing is just to tell someone that you're having trouble. You don't need to tell everyone in your life your private business. Maybe tell your family that you're having a hard time financially. Tell them that you can't keep your house clean or drive yourself places anymore. You might be surprised at the help that's offered.

Index

ABOUT THE AUTHOR

Amy has spent most of her legal career helping people obtain Social Security disability benefits. Amy was born and raised in Phoenix, Arizona. She attended Carnegie Mellon University in Pittsburgh, Pennsylvania, earning her Bachelor's of Arts in Psychology. Amy graduated in 2000 with college and university honors. After college, Amy returned to Arizona to attend the University of Arizona James E. Rogers College of Law.

Continuing her passion for disability law, Amy has given a number of continuing legal education seminars on Social Security for other attorneys and members of the community. If you would like Amy to speak to your organization, please contact her office.

Amy is married and lives in Phoenix with her husband. You can follow her on twitter @fosterlawaz or go to her website at http://fosterlawaz.com where she continues to blog about disability topics and tries to find and post more resources for the disabled.